Unwin Education Books: 33

THE DEVELOPMENT OF MEANING

Unwin Education Books

Series Editor: Ivor Morrish, B.D., B.A., Dip.Ed. (London), B.A. (Bristol)

Unwin Education Books: 33
Series Editor: Ivor Morrish

The Development
of Meaning
A Study of Children's
Use of Language

JOAN TOUGH
M.A., Ph.D.

Senior Lecturer in Education
Institute of Education, University of Leeds

London

GEORGE ALLEN & UNWIN LTD

RUSKIN HOUSE   MUSEUM STREET

First published in 1977

© George Allen & Unwin (Publishers) Ltd, 1977

ISBN 0 04 372020 X hardback
      0 04 372021 8 paperback

Printed in Great Britain
in 10/11 pt Times Roman type
by John Wright & Sons Ltd, at the Stonebridge Press, Bristol

Acknowledgements

I am grateful to all those who, by offering advice, giving time for discussion, or by practical help, forwarded the work of the project. In particular, I must thank my colleagues Betty Glossop and Elizabeth Sestini for their able assistance.

My thanks are also due to the parents, teachers and children whose willing co-operation made the study possible, and to Margaret Metcalfe-Smith, formerly Lecturer in Education, in the Institute of Education, University of Leeds, without whose advice and encouragement this study would never have come into being.

Contents

PART I

Chapter 1

Introduction: The Language and Environment Project

In January 1965 I was appointed to the University of Leeds Institute of Education to undertake research and contribute to a post-experience course in education.

During the previous five years I had taught in a College of Education which specialised in preparing teachers for nursery and primary schools. During this period I had seen the work of a number of nursery schools, and I had also become aware of the great problems facing primary schools which serve areas made up almost entirely of lower-working-class families. Such schools were to be found not only around the city centre, where the majority of children came from the long rows of back-to-back houses, with their narrow cobbled or unsurfaced streets, but also from the more spacious surroundings of the council housing estates on the perimeter of the city, particularly where the policy was to build schools which would almost entirely serve the estate's population. I came to realise how great the problems were for the teachers, and for the students on teaching practice, in these schools.

During this period I became thoroughly familiar with the problems of both children who were at disadvantage and teachers who worked with them. At the same time, I was becoming aware of the way in which language appears to facilitate much of the learning that is expected to go on in school. I had long been familiar with Piaget's work on children's thinking but now I met Vygotsky's and Luria's and then Bernstein's work: these raised for me new questions about the influence of the linguistic experiences to which the child is exposed during his early years.

My whole experience during this period led me to ask whether the educational disadvantage of many children might, to some extent, be a reflection of their disadvantage in the linguistic environment of school and not only the reflection of the social and material environment of their homes. It led me also to wonder whether experience in a nursery school might help to redress the child's social and material disadvantage and, perhaps more important, might offer these children opportunities to develop ways of using language which seem to be the necessary equipment for benefiting fully from the school experiences to follow. In the light of research and discussion of the whole question of learning in the early years which has come to the fore since this time, the questions which I put forward as a basis from which to set up a research project were perhaps oversimplified, and this became evident as the work proceeded and new insights were gained.

The Longitudinal Study

The basis of the research was to be a close study of the language used by selected groups of children from an early age onwards. So that the effects of nursery education might be considered, children were to be selected at the age of 3 years, when it would be known whether the child was to have nursery education or not.

Since all studies of language in use produce large quantities of data, the maximum number of children to be included in the study was set at sixty-four. The data which form the basis of this study were collected from a population of sixty-four children, thirty-two of whom had entered nursery schools or classes at the time of selection, and a further thirty-two children who were not expected to have nursery education. These children were to be seen again in school at the ages of $5\frac{1}{2}$ years and $7\frac{1}{2}$ years.

THE 'ADVANTAGED' AND 'DISADVANTAGED' DISTINCTION

In order to study the effects of home environment on children's development and use of language, the parents (one or both) of half the children selected followed professions which are generally reached through a course in higher education, that is they were teachers, doctors, lawyers and others of similar status. The parents of the remainder of the children had completed their education at the minimum age, and worked in unskilled or semi-skilled occupations.

The children for the study, then, were drawn from these two sections of the population and were between the ages of 3 and $3\frac{1}{2}$ years at the time at which their talk was first recorded.

Since there is much evidence to show that children of parents in the professions have a much greater chance of achieving the maximum benefit from our educational system, by staying at school and continuing into higher education, than children from unskilled or semi-skilled workers, the groups were considered to have been drawn from populations which were, in relation to one another, at advantage or disadvantage within education. These groups are referred to throughout the book as *advantaged* and *disadvantaged*, but the reader is asked to bear in mind that we refer to the position known to exist *within education* for the children from these sections of the population. (For some of the evidence of the inequality in education the reader might refer to Douglas, 1964; Douglas, Ross and Simpson, 1968; Wiseman, 1964.)

OTHER CRITERIA FOR SELECTION

Since of necessity the number of children selected for this study was to be small, it seemed essential to take into account several factors which might contribute to differences in the development of language and stem from causes other than differences in the experiences of using language offered to children by their homes.

Many studies have shown that there is a close association between measured intelligence and language development. It seemed important not to include children in the study whose basic ability might later be considered to be the main factor limiting language development. The lower limit for inclusion in the sample was therefore set at IQ 105 as measured by the Stanford Binet Scale of Intelligence (1960 revision). Since there is also a good deal of evidence to show that children from large families tend to score less on language tests than others, no child was included from a family that had more than six children. There is also evidence to suggest that rejection and emotional stress are likely to affect both the general intellectual achievement and the development of language, and so children were not included where there were known or suspected conditions likely to lead to such problems.

No child was included whose mother did not speak English as her first language and West Indian children were not included because of problems that might arise from their use of non-standard English. In the end all the children selected came from the indigenous population. No child was included who was shy or withdrawn or hostile to the observer, since such conditions might prevent a view being gained of the child's real ability to use language. It was also felt that children for the nursery groups should be happily settled in school when their use of language was recorded, since a representative sample of talk might otherwise not be obtained. Of necessity children were included only if they spoke clearly enough for transcriptions to be made of what they said.

SELECTING THE NURSERY GROUP

The children who were attending nursery school were expected to stay until they moved to an infants' school and all the nursery schools and classes from which the children were drawn were in the charge of qualified teachers.

The head teachers of nursery schools and classes were asked to introduce the author to mothers of children who fitted the criteria for selection. The author then visited the home to seek permission to study the child and to gain essential information from the parent. The collection of the data from these groups of children was spread over one year and in the following year data were collected from groups of children who were not expected to have nursery education.

SELECTING THE GROUPS WITHOUT NURSERY SCHOOL EXPERIENCE

To distinguish the groups, those children without experience in nursery school are referred to as in 'non-nursery' groups. In order to select these groups, approaches were made to several head teachers of infants' schools which served areas where it was known that there were no nursery schools or nursery classes available. These schools served the large housing estates on the edge of the city, or the 'down town' areas of the city. The head teachers were asked to introduce the author to families that appeared to fit the criteria laid down for inclusion as disadvantaged and that had a child who would reach his third birthday during the following twelve months, and who was likely, eventually, to come to the school.

It proved to be unexpectedly difficult to find children who would not have some form of pre-school experience, in either nursery or playgroup, for the 'professional' group. Even when children were found who, it seemed, would not attend nursery or playgroup, there was no guarantee that they would not do so if places became available later. It would seem that many parents in the professional group see nursery education as beneficial in some way.

All the mothers were then visited, and the children were seen in their own homes. The child's general ability and responsiveness were observed and once information about the parents' occupation and education had been checked, it was possible to decide whether the child was likely to be suitable for inclusion. Arrangements were then made for further interviews, either at school or at home, whichever the mother preferred. Because selection of nursery education might be a reflection of other attitudes that might be important in the context of the study, no child was selected whose mother would not have wished him to have nursery education if a place had been available.

THE DISADVANTAGED GROUPS

As decisions were made about the composition of the group described as 'disadvantaged', it became clear that the criteria for selection had already excluded the most disadvantaged section of the population. We had failed to recognise that it is precisely those families that are confronted with difficulties, that is where there are many children and perhaps the loss of a parent, or a breakdown in family relations, or the ill health of one or both parents, as well as insecurity and material poverty, that tend to provide the least favourable environments in which a child can grow up. Nevertheless, the terms 'disadvantaged' and 'advantaged' were appropriate, since they described the relative positions the children from these sections of the population clearly have within school.

THE SELECTED GROUPS

During the two years of the first phase of the project four groups of sixteen children were established, with eight boys and eight girls in each. Two of these groups satisfied the criteria for description as 'advantaged' and two for description as 'disadvantaged'. One advantaged group and one disadvantaged group were expected to have two years in nursery school, and the other two were not expected to have such experience.

The problems of establishing matched groups are well known and no more is claimed than that the groups appeared to be so close on all variables that appeared to be relevant that making comparisons between them seemed justified. Information about the composition of the groups at the time of the first recording is given in Table 1 in the Appendix on page 180. The groups for comparison throughout the study were kept at twelve. Data were collected from the additional sixteen children who were to provide replacements for children in the original groups who might become inaccessible at later stages. Wherever possible, children who left the area were followed up in the area to which they had moved. In this way it was possible to compare data from forty-eight children at each stage.

Sampling Children's Language: A Basis for Comparison

The intention of the study was, then, to compare the language used by four selected groups of children when they were 3 years old and then again at $5\frac{1}{2}$ and $7\frac{1}{2}$ years of age. This meant that the data were collected in three phases each lasting two years.

Making a comparison of the language used by children, whether between children, or of the language of a child at different ages, poses a major problem: it depends upon finding some reliable observable evidence of the child's capability in using language. There are now a number of tests available that are designed to be used with young children and that might together be expected to cover a wide range of skills. However, tests were rejected as a means of investigation at the outset, since it was felt that it might be difficult to ensure the co-operation of some 3-year-olds and to persuade them that it was important that their best efforts should be seen.

But tests were rejected also because it was felt that it was important to discover the way in which the child was disposed to use language, since this, it seemed, might be the important issue in considering whether the child's development and use of language might be a crucial factor in determining the way in which he could respond to, and profit from, the experiences offered to him in school.

If the child's skill in using language is to be observed and assessed in some way, and tests are not to be used, then it follows that the child must be persuaded or provoked to talk or write, or otherwise act upon the spoken or written word to show that he comprehends it: or he must be observed in situations where his speech flows naturally in spontaneous response to his own or his companions' activities. In the case of the 3-year-old child, observing his talk and his responses to talk are the only possible alternatives open to investigation.

But deciding whether to question the child, or observe how he can respond to talk, or eavesdrop on his spontaneous talk, does not settle the problem; for the way in which questions are asked, the topics about which they are asked and the presence of other people may all affect the way in which the child will respond. If it is decided to collect his spontaneous talk, then it is possible that there will be differences in the way in which he talks between one situation and another. If he is with other children the composition of the group may influence what he will say. Even the way in which he uses language with other children may be different if an adult is known to be listening, and it may be different again if the adult enters into a conversation with him when the group is present.

Still another problem faces those who study children's language. Whether the sample of his language is obtained by asking the child questions, talking with him or eavesdropping on his talk with others, it is clear that what is being observed is what he finds appropriate to do with his language in that particular situation. Although evidence will be gained of many things he can do with his language, it may not show *all* that he can do with language. But probing to find the limits of the child's knowledge of language will not indicate, either, the way in which he is *disposed* to use language, that is the habitual mode of responding that has been established, and this may be the crucial factor.

A major problem then was to decide on the kind of situation that should be used, when the children were 3 years old, for observing and recording their use of language. But once the situation in which the child's use of language was to be sampled had been decided, there still remained the problem of how to make comparisons between the collected samples. This meant looking for measures of some kind, or establishing criteria by which the language recorded might be classified. This, perhaps, became the biggest problem; although all would agree that what the child does with his language is an important aspect to examine, most studies in the end have relied upon measurable features of the structure of the child's speech for making comparisons and, for the most part, meaning has been neglected.

Devising a method of making a comparison of the language used by different children that took into account the kinds of meaning that were in evidence became a major feature in the development of the study, and provides the basis for the arguments put forward in the following chapters.

SAMPLING THE CHILDREN'S LANGUAGE AT THE AGE OF 3

Finally, it was decided that the sampling of the 3-year-old's use of language should be done as the child played with his chosen companion with a collection of play materials which would be the same for all. A trial run with children not included in the project's selected groups showed that the materials would stimulate play and that children were likely to be motivated to use language freely. The observer's role was seen as one of giving support and encouragement to the children as they played and not one of trying to provoke the child to use language for particular purposes. It was argued that the child was likely to reveal his general disposition to use language in this kind of situation, provided that the recording continued for a considerable length of time. The children's talk in the play situation was recorded for an hour, or until he wished to leave the observation room. In only a few cases were the recordings less than an hour, and none was less than three-quarters of an hour.

SAMPLING THE CHILDREN'S LANGUAGE AT THE AGES OF 5 AND 7

At the later stages, that is when the children reached the ages of $5\frac{1}{2}$ and then $7\frac{1}{2}$ years, interviews with the child were recorded that centred on the use of a range of materials in situations that required the child to use language for purposes that it seems are essential in education. It was expected that data of this kind would provide a basis for comparisons to be made between children, which was also likely to provide some insights into the problems that some children have in responding to experiences offered to them in school. The rationale for selecting, designing and conducting particular interview situations will be discussed at appropriate places in the text.

RECORDING CHILDREN'S LANGUAGE

The most formidable aspect of studying children's use of language in natural settings is the sheer volume of material that accumulates. We soon came to appreciate how much simpler the task would have been had we relied on language tests for making comparisons. On the other hand as the tedious business of transcribing hours of tape recordings proceeded, we became more and more convinced that tests could not have reflected the tremendous versatility in the use of language which we were observing in our 3-year-olds. Whether we should ever succeed in finding methods of analysis that would reflect this versatility was a matter that gave us great concern from the outset. The methods that were well known at that stage revealed their inadequacies as soon as we began to apply them.

We found that, because the same set of materials were used in every play session, there were themes that recurred in the recordings. The presence of particular toys, for example small cars and a fire engine, a family of small dolls with furniture and house play accessories, including a telephone, tended to stimulate particular kinds of imaginative and role play.

At the same time, however, it was clear that the informal atmosphere in which the recordings were made allowed the children to follow their inclinations to draw on their own personal experiences. The role played by the author was one that did not set out to lead or stimulate children to follow any particular form of play, but one that provided the children with a supportive, accepting audience. Every effort was made to play the same role with all the children. From time to time, small emergencies arose, for examples, disputes over the use of the play materials, and accidents typical of children's play. On examining the transcriptions when all recordings had been made, it was felt that any effects from such emergencies would be similarly distributed throughout the groups to be compared.

At the end of two years we had a large collection of data and we looked for methods of analysis that would help us to identify any differences between the groups, which existed at that stage, in the language used by the children during the recorded play sessions.

We turned to examine the structure of the child's spoken language first because it provided one aspect that could be examined objectively and also because we could find no other way to begin. In this it seems we were in good company: much of the recent work on children's language has begun, and also ended, with the study of the structural features of the language produced by the child.

Finally, it perhaps should be made clear that the author writes as a teacher whose interest in language originates from an interest in child development. We tread warily in the field of language study, for, like many others, we are still groping towards an understanding of the language phenomenon and trying to draw upon the insights that are offered by linguistic theory.

In preparing this account of the longitudinal study, our main aim has been to convince those who are concerned with the education of the young child of the contribution that a study of language can make to our understanding of the young child's cognitive and social development, and of the problems that many children have in interpreting the experiences they meet in school.

Chapter 2

The Development of Language: from First Words to Complex Utterances

First Words

One fact stands out quite clearly about the 3-year-olds in the Language and Environment project: they had all learned a great deal about using language already. Although their voices were immature, and there were some problems of articulation, nevertheless no one could doubt that they were all effectively using language as a means of communicating with others.

This feat of learning, which all normal children accomplish by their fourth year, is frequently taken for granted by teachers and parents. Although parents may take pleasure in the first words their babies utter, and may boast of the prowess of their young children in talking, they will also be quick to feel that something is wrong with a child who has not begun to talk much by the age of 3. And yet to master the complex structures of language at an age when he would not be able to understand the principles of operation if they were explained to him must stand as one of man's most remarkable achievements. This learning appears all the more impressive, perhaps, when we consider that it is achieved in little more than a year from the time when the child first utters two words in sequence with the intention of expressing particular meanings.

The children in the project provided an illustration of what would seem to be the general pattern of development. A structured interview with each child's mother was taken when the child was about to be included in the project's population. Mothers were at that time asked to recall particular stages of the child's development. From their replies there appeared to be little difference reported in development between the groups of children. Every mother recalled that her child had some 'words' at 12 months old. Their estimates varied from 'three or four' to 'about twelve', but there was no significant difference in the distribution between the groups. The majority of the sixty-four mothers interviewed reported that the child first put together two words just before or just after his second birthday. Eight reported that their children had done this between the ages of 18 months and 21 months (six of these early talkers were girls), whilst fourteen thought that the child was rather later than this, and estimated the age at which the child used two words together as late as 26 to 30 months. Several mothers in the educationally disadvantaged groups made their estimate with less confidence than others and several pointed out that where the child was one of a family of four or five it was difficult to remember his progress unless it was very different from the others in the family.

It is not, of course, that the baby's first words suddenly erupt with no preparation, as it were. During the first months of life the baby progressively differentiates his experiences as his motor control increases. He is gradually able to take up a range of postures, move himself from place to place, and co-ordinate the use of hands and eyes as a means of exploring aspects of the world around him. During this period his voice also comes more and more under his control and he discovers that the different sounds he utters produce different responses from the people around him. Since people are expecting his vocalisations to carry meaning, they are quick to respond to and infer meaning from any sound the baby makes which carries any resemblance to a word.

In this way the baby's own development, and the expectations of his parents and others, lead to the emergence of his first 'words', that is sounds which are made consistently in response to similar objects or situations and which are interpreted and responded to consistently as carrying this reference. Such 'words' may first occur towards the end of the first year, but it seems generally that it may not be until the middle of the second year that the child begins to use these 'words' with an intention to communicate.

Although there must always have been those who have wondered how the child can develop language at so early an age, it is only in recent years that this period of life has come to the fore as an area for close study and research. In this country Lewis's early work stands alone as a detailed description of the way in which the child learns to speak (Lewis, 1957). The baby's first word-like utterances, which are made to carry a range of meanings through the use of different patterns of intonation, are seen as a tool which helps him to differentiate his experiences further, as the responses he draws from adults lead him to extend the basis for classification which is developing.

For example, the child may produce a sound that resembles the word 'ball' and demonstrate by his responses that both his own and the adult's use of the word is understood in reference to his own particular ball. He may from time to time use the word when he sees other balls, or ball-like objects. The adult's response to his efforts will lead the child to separate those objects that are to be included in the category 'ball' and those that are to be excluded. When he uses the term as he reaches for an orange the adult is likely to use the relevant term 'orange' and perhaps will give him experiences of the taste and smell, and of actions which are not associated with 'ball'. When he points to the moon and says 'ball' he is likely to be told 'No it's not a ball, it's the moon', perhaps with explanations that can mean little to him. He may nevertheless not only learn to exclude the moon from his use of the word 'ball', and to use the term 'moon' for this particular experience that occurs regularly and consistently; he may even learn that 'moon' is not always ball-like.

But these early word-like utterances are capable of carrying a range of meanings and are not limited to acting as reference to objects or actions only. The 'word' may at different times carry one of a range of social meanings; it may serve to protest or command, to cajole or admire, to inform or question, as it is produced with particular tones of voice and intonation pattern and is accompanied by gestures and action. The listening adult looks for clues to the baby's intention and then responds on the basis of the interpretation he has made.

The intention to 'mean' can be seen to be the essential feature of these primitive words, or 'holophrases', and they would seem to have the potential for holding a range of meanings that provide the impetus that carries the baby towards differentiating and acquiring the structures of his mother tongue. Michael Halliday, in studying the early words used by his son Nigel, comes to the conclusion that the social functions of language have their origin in these holophrases and he sees the functions which they serve becoming vested in the emerging structures of the child's speech, (Halliday, 1973, p. 37). We shall discuss this possibility in a later chapter.

The period that follows, during which the child's language develops so rapidly, and he demonstrates an ability to acquire linguistic structures, although still at an age when explanations of grammatical rules can mean little to him, has come to fascinate both linguists and psychologists during recent years.

The speech of the children in the study, which was recorded when they were 3 years old, provides an illustration of the rapidity with which this learning is accomplished. It might be expected that, since the child is no more than 18 months, and perhaps even as little as 6 months, away from the period of the holophrase at the age of 3 to $3\frac{1}{2}$ years, many would still have a long way to go before the basic rules of adult speech are established. Yet this was not found to be the case in the groups of 3-year-olds in the study. Although many of them had some problems of articulation that gave their speech the character of immaturity, it was clear that they had all established a wide range of basic structures of English.

All the children produced utterances which were not 'well formed' according to the requirements of the grammar but it was clear that sometimes these were 'errors', since they demonstrated that they could use the structure correctly on other occasions. For example, all children were usually making agreements of number and only rarely failed to use a plural agreement, but they would use a plural agreement form which was not needed, or use the regular form when an irregular form was applicable. The persistent 'errors' came from the application of the regular past tense ending when an irregular past tense should have been used and from the omission of auxiliaries in the extension of the verb, for example 'He going home'.

Children from all the groups had some problems in making agreements and using past tenses. Children from the disadvantaged groups however made more 'errors', although some of these were, in fact, likely to be 'correct' according to the model from which they had learned, for example the reversal of the rule for using 'was' and 'were' to indicate singular and plural. They also had more articulation problems, but only one child persistently used babyisms, for example 'me' instead of 'I', 'bye-byes' for sleep. The most striking characteristic of the language of all the 3-year-olds in the study was the closeness to the 'adult' form which they all displayed.

This picture may not be typical of all 3-year-olds, however, for the criteria for selection had been that all children should be talking readily and clearly enough for the observer to be able to identify what the child was saying. Children may not have been considered as suitable by teachers if they were still at the 'telegraphic' stage, that is where the embedding structures of speech were not yet developing.

There was no evidence from the study to suggest that children who were educationally disadvantaged talked any less than those from the professional groups. Children varied in the number of utterances they produced; the range was from 87 utterances to 300 utterances, but the range of differences was about the same for all groups. Again this may not reflect the position with respect to the whole population, but may stem from the criteria on which children were selected for the study.

At the age of 3 it is to be expected that some complex structures are not likely to be used, and that there will be many errors caused by failure to apply grammatical rules. No child, for example, used a full passive construction, although constructions like 'He got runned over' were used frequently. All children were able to use negative constructions, for example 'I've not got one', though often there was an omission of the contracted 'have' to give 'I not got one'. Few children used constructions of the form 'I've got no cars', but more frequently used the form 'I've not got some cars'.

All the 3-year-olds in the study asked some questions and although the range and types of questions were limited, and there were differences between the groups on the range used, they all showed that they could apply the inversion rule. For example they asked 'What is that?' not 'What that is?' and all asked questions in the form 'Is that yours?' although the form 'That's yours?', in which tone of voice indicates the question, was used, but this in any case is a use made familiar by adults, particularly with the tag 'is it?' or 'isn't it?'. All the children used tags of this kind and some children used this feature frequently.

Although the child's production of particular structures and his problems in using the grammatical rules were of interest, making an analysis of these features as a basis for comparing the groups did not seem likely to bring the most valuable insights into the importance of any differences that might be developing. We sought a basis for making comparisons that would reflect any differences that existed between the groups in their ability to use language, rather than differences in their ability to observe grammatical rules. In order to do this we turned first of all to methods that had been well tried in the past.

The Structural Complexity of the Utterances of 3-Year-Olds

Forty years ago there had already developed amongst psychologists in the United States considerable interest in children's language, and the analysis of certain structural features of speech had already been recognised as a means of comparing the language of groups of children. These measures included the analysis of vocabulary, the computation of the mean length of a number of utterances, and the relative frequency with which particular types of words were used.

This development culminated in Mildred Templin's descriptive study of the inter-relations of the articulation of speech sounds, sound discrimination, vocabulary and sentence structure. The traditional units of word, clause and sentence were taken as a basis for comparing the complexity of the language used by groups of children between the ages of 3 and 8 years, selected as a representative sample of the urban population in the USA (Templin, 1957).

In Templin's study the mean length of a number of sentences produced by children in devised situations proved to be a measure that discriminated between children from different socio-economic groups, as well as between different ages and different levels of intelligence. The Templin study showed that the mean length of the sentences produced by the child increased with age, but higher mean length was also found to be associated with higher intelligence and higher socio-economic group. The classification of the complexity of the sentences used also revealed a similar association between greater complexity and increased age, higher intelligence and higher socio-economic group.

The protocols used by Templin for recognising the unit for measurement were adapted for the analysis of the more extensive data of the Language and Environment project. The concept of the 'complete sentence' used by Mildred Templin was abandoned since this would have neglected a large proportion of the data. In informal conversations, in any case, speakers do not necessarily conform to the notion of completeness, i.e. having a complete subject and predicate according to the rules of grammar. Three-year-olds clearly are not aware of 'grammaticality' and frequently fail to make 'complete' sentences. 'Complete' utterances, that is utterances that clearly have a completeness for the child, even though grammatically there are elements missing, were taken as the unit for analysis. All the child's utterances, except those that were incomplete because they defied transcription, or because the child was interrupted or broke off speaking, formed the data to be analysed. Any identical repetitions of utterances were excluded from the data and so were lines of nursery rhymes and verse. Measures of utterance length and of complexity in the structure of the utterances were then used to compare the language used by the groups of children in the project.

MEASURES OF UTTERANCE LENGTH

The mean length of all the utterances produced by each child was calculated and the groups were compared using a Mann–Whitney U test (a test that takes into account the rank order of children's scores and is not based on a comparison of total scores of the groups). The differences between the advantaged and disadvantaged groups was found to be at a level of significance beyond 0·001 and there was little overlap in the scores made by individual children in the two groups. One child only from the disadvantaged group ranked higher than some children in the advantaged groups. The mean length of all the utterances produced by the advantaged groups was 5·7 words and by the disadvantaged groups 4·0 words.

In both groups the mean scores for girls and boys tended to be very close. In the case of both the advantaged and the disadvantaged groups the mean scores of the children attending nursery schools and classes were higher than those not attending.

In addition it was found that the mean length of the five longest utterances produced by each child, and the number of utterances produced by each child that were longer than eight words, also differentiated the advantaged groups from the disadvantaged groups. Table 2 in the Appendix gives these and other results.

COMPLEXITY OF THE STRUCTURE OF UTTERANCES

The method described by Templin for analysing the complexity of the structure of sentences was adapted as a means of classifying the children's complete utterances. All utterances were examined and classified on the following basis.

1 Simple utterances, that is without the use of clauses or elaborating phrases, e.g.
    I've got a red car.
    Michele's going to hit me.
    It's only a little man in there.

2 Compound utterances, where two or more simple utterances are joined by 'and' without a pause indicating a new intention, e.g.

There's a cowboy and an Indian and a see-saw and they're shooting each other dead.

3 Complex utterances, where two or more simple utterances are joined with a dependency relationship of some kind, usually by using the conjunctions 'but', 'so', 'because', 'if' and 'although', or where a clause of some kind is used or an elaborating phrase, e.g.

If you shake it up and down all the snow goes over everything.

The doctor'll give her a pink thing that will make her better.

4 Elaborated utterances, where two or more of the features required for judgement as a complex utterance appear, e.g.

I'm going to get a new coat but it'll have to be bigger than this one or else I can't wear it.

RESULTS OF THE ANALYSIS OF STRUCTURAL COMPLEXITY OF UTTERANCES

Using this method of analysis the groups were differentiated by the tendency towards the use of the more complex forms of utterances by the advantaged group. Few elaborated utterances were used, but the children in the advantaged groups were using clauses much more frequently than those in the disadvantaged groups. In fact, it can be seen from Table 3 in the Appendix, page 182, that the advantaged groups used more complex structures more than four times as often as the disadvantaged groups. It can also be seen that the advantaged groups used clauses almost five times as frequently as the disadvantaged groups. Adverbial clauses (not shown in Table 3) that refer to cause–effect relationships are used on sixty-three occasions by children in the advantaged groups but there are only three instances in the talk of the twenty-four children in the disadvantaged groups.

This first analysis revealed that there were already differences between the children in the advantaged and those in the disadvantaged groups, in the length and in the complexity of the utterances which they produced. Clearly, it might be expected that greater complexity in the structure of the utterances would lead to longer utterances. But although it was established that the advantaged group used complexity in the structuring of utterances more frequently, complexity of this kind was not the general characteristic of the major part of 3-year-olds' talk and perhaps did not explain the wide differences between the groups in the length of utterances. Other explanations were sought and the effect that particular features which lie within utterances might have on the mean length of utterances was considered next.

Chapter 3

The Development of Complexity within Children's Utterances

The rate at which the child acquires language and his ability to observe the rules of grammar are not the only aspects of the child's use of language that have fascinated linguists and psychologists during recent years. Above all, it is the tremendous versatility with which the young child uses language to produce utterances that he is likely never to have heard before that has come in for a good deal of discussion. This versatility has been described as 'creativeness' on the part of the child, since he continually produces utterances that he has neither heard before nor produced before.

It is the problem of finding explanations to account for this 'creativeness' that has provoked the development of a theory of language acquisition that assigns to the child innate formulae for acquiring language, and has led to the development of the concept of 'generative' grammar. A good generative grammar is one that will, as the term suggests, generate all the possible sentences, and only those sentences, in the language that an adult native speaker of the language would recognise as 'well formed'.

The development of the concept of generative grammar, particularly Noam Chomsky's major contribution (Chomsky, 1965), has strongly influenced the study of children's language over the last ten years. In the first place, it is argued, the speed of language acquisition is dependent on the child being able to acquire and operate rules, rules that it seems are innate, since children the world over seem to go through the same rule-making sequences, and in the early stages of acquiring any language they try to use the same procedures. For example, although Russian is a strongly inflected language, where word order has little importance, children at first order their words on the model 'actor–action–acted upon' in the same way that we see children ordering their first utterances in English.

The explanation of such universal phenomena rests, Chomsky argues, in the 'language universals' that underlie all languages. This universality resides in the 'deep structure' on which the capacity for language is grounded, and which might be regarded as the innate concepts of language, that is, the categories of signs, noun and verb, which match the categories of actor, action and acted upon, and of the formula that links them in this order, that is the sentence. These universals underlie all well-formed sentences in any language, and every language has developed some means of elaborating on these universals. These elaborations result from operations, which are referred to as *transformations*, that also are drawn from the universal principles of permutation in the ordering of words, and of the addition and deletion of elements. The rules that are derived from these transformational universals are themselves unique to each language, but beneath any surface structure in any language lies a deep structure that, Chomsky argues, is an active proposition consisting of a noun phrase and a verb phrase. When the transformational rules of a particular language are applied a surface structure that is unique to that language is produced.

Generative grammar, with its focus on phrase structures and transformational rules, has offered a tool for investigating language which has been seized upon and used as though it derived from a psychological rather than a linguistic theory. The result has been an inclination to see the child's acquisition of language in terms of a developing sequence of grammars, which embody universal rules and which, by stages, lead to the establishment of the adult grammar. Such study generally assigns the initiative in development to the child's ability to construct his own rules, and to apply them to produce linguistic forms that reflectively promote his intentions to communicate.

The almost inevitable outcome of this work is the postulation of innate mechanisms to account for the acquisition of language. McNeil has termed this mechanism the Language Acquisition Device (LAD) (McNeil, 1966a, 1966b and 1970) and places this at the centre of a theory of the genetic development of language in children. McNeil discusses the way in which speech, produced by the application of the innate grammar, relates to meaning. McNeil, like Halliday, sees the origins of linguistic structure lying in the 'holophrasic' speech of the young child. The child's holophrases are themselves autonomous but since they have the intention of reference behind them, they begin to lead to communication that is not entirely dependent on the adult's empathy for interpretation. McNeil argues that these holophrasic, referential utterances are, as it were, the predicate to a subject implied by the situational context, so that he concludes that the concept of a sentence as a set of grammatical relations is developed long before transformations make elaborations possible.

To begin with, grammatical relations are implicit within the child's utterances, and then patterned speech begins to emerge with two-word combinations, controlled by a grammar that contains two classes, the 'open' and the 'pivot' class of words. Pivot words act as modifiers on a range of words, typically nouns, that belong to the open class. For example, at some point the child masters the articulation and meaning of the word 'gone'. This he uses as a pivot word, that is one that he can combine with a number of other words to produce, for example, 'Mummy gone', 'Daddy gone', 'Milk gone', 'Car gone'. With a small number of pivot words and a growing number of words that can be combined with them or with each other, the possibilities for the child of intentional communication grow rapidly.

McNeil tests the hypothesis that the child progresses by adopting a series of new grammars from which emerges, somewhere after the age of 2 years, a rudimentary phrase structure grammar. This phrase structure grammar is based on the grammatical universals of subject–predicate, verb–object and modifier and head noun. According to McNeil, the child progressively adopts new phrase structure rules and new transformational rules by which the underlying sentence is elaborated to become the utterance.

The concept of 'transformation', then, is central to a generative grammar; put simply, it refers to each change that must be made to the underlying 'sentence', consisting of a noun phrase and a verb phrase, in order to produce an utterance in which particular features of speech show the relationships between parts of the sentence required by the grammar. In English, for example, there are the transformational rules that govern inflections, for example the suffix 's' may result from the operation of one or another of three transformational rules. The 's' is added to a word in order to express 'plural', or to express 'possession', in both of which it relates one word to another. Then again it is used to make agreement in the third person singular of a verb, that is, it relates the noun phrase to the verb phrase.

Other transformational rules are applied to the verbs to indicate the continuous present by the ending 'ing' or the past by the ending 'ed', or the re-ordering of words to give the question form, that is the inversion of subject and verb.

How do children come to master these transformational rules? Brown and Hanlon (1970), in considering whether the acquisition of transformational rules is directly related to the complexity of the derivation of the forms of grammatical structure, suggest that transformational grammar is not only a description of linguistic knowledge but also has psychological actuality. But testing the hypothesis that forms are acquired in order of the derivational complexity is complicated by the fact that the child is exposed, through the parents' talk, to some forms more frequently than to others. It is also found that young children often use a complex form that has been learnt as though it were a single word. For example, 'What's that?' occurs early as a single learned response; but later the child may begin to apply a current grammar, and say 'What that is?' and this might be seen as an advance, even though it does not result in a 'well-formed' sentence, because it is nevertheless generated by a grammar. In time the child will produce 'What's that?' once more, but now through the application of the rule, by which means it can now be seen to have become an integrated part of the grammar.

Transformational generative grammar has, then, given impetus to the study of the child's acquisition of language. It has challenged the view that learning of language at this early age is a passive affair, and is in sharp contrast to the behaviourist view put forward by Skinner (1957) that language consists of a set of habits acquired by imitation, which encompasses a collection of words, in learned sequences of phrases and sentences.

But what insights has transformational grammar provided for the study of children's language? It has perhaps brought a new understanding of the 'errors' that children make as they use language, seeing these as failures to apply the transformational rules. In some studies a comparison of 'errors' has provided a basis for comparing the language produced by children. Paula Menyuk's work is perhaps the most extensive of these. She traces the sequence in which the rules are mastered by examining the errors made by children at various ages (Menyuk, 1963).

In a study of the ability of children between 5 and 10 years to use particular linguistic structures, Carol Chomsky has shown that structures which on the surface appear to be very similar offer problems of different degrees of intensity that are related to the complexity of the transformations that are required to produce the sentence, that is the derivational complexity (Chomsky, 1969). This work is of interest, since it shows that, although it is clear that by the age of 5 most children may have mastered the basic structures of the language and may approximate very closely to the adult form, there are still structures that they are unlikely to use themselves and that may cause problems of understanding when used by others.

Neither of the approaches referred to above, however, seemed to offer a useful approach to the analysis of the internal structure of the utterances produced by the children in the study. But transformational grammar also indicates ways of evaluating the child's demonstrated knowledge of the structures of language. This can be done by considering the transformations that have been made to an underlying 'kernel' sentence in order to produce the surface structure that is elaborated in each utterance. The gradual increase of the length of utterances that takes place as the child moves from the 'telegraphic' form of utterance to the 'adult' form, that is, to the 'well-formed' utterance, results, it would seem, from the transformations made to the basic elements of the 'kernel' sentence, that is, in the elaboration of the noun and verb phrases. It would seem to follow, then, that an examination of the complexity of the noun and verb phrases used by the children would reflect the control they had already acquired over the operation of transformations.

Courtney Cazden, in a study of the effectiveness of two different strategies used for promoting children's development of language, has devised measures of the elaboration of noun and verb phrases, basing them on the number of transformations in operation (Cazden, 1965). These measures reflect the insights gained from transformational grammar and are based on scores given for the application of each transformation: for example, in the case of the noun phrase scores are given for the application of the rules of agreement that indicate plurality, and for each modifier used in the noun phrase; that is, each adjective, adjectival phrase, article and possessive inflection present in the noun phrase is scored.

In the verb phrase, the application of the rules of agreement between subject and verb, the inflections or verb endings, the use of auxiliaries, and the use of modals, which together allow particular time perspectives or degree of possibility and tentativity to be expressed, are all scored with a weighting towards transformations that denote greater complexity or subtlety of meaning. Some exceptions were made in the hierarchy of derivational complexity where there was evidence that the structures were acquired early by all children, for example 'got' appears early and does not necessarily reflect a transformation from 'get'.

Thus the scores given to noun or verb phrases are generally based on the number of transformations that have been applied in order to produce the particular surface structure from the underlying elements of the 'kernel' sentence.

The study by Courtney Cazden, however, included children below the age of 3 years and from a deprived black population, so the measures used needed to be considerably extended to accommodate the generally greater maturity of the children in the Language and Environment project.

Complexity in the Noun Phrase

The scale constructed for measuring the complexity within the noun phrase is given in the Appendix, page 183: it ranges from a score of one for a noun standing alone, to a score of six where the noun is accompanied by several modifiers, and includes scores for each plural or possessive inflection. Although none of the children in the project produced noun phrases that scored more than six, there were many more noun phrases which scored six than in the Cazden data, when only one noun phrase scoring six was recorded.

Cazden calculated the mean score of all the noun phrases used by a child: this is referred to as the Noun Phrase (instance) Index. Using this index to compare the groups, it is clear that the children in the advantaged groups generally produce higher indices than those in the disadvantaged groups: this difference is found to be at a high level of statistical significance. The nursery disadvantaged group has higher indices than the disadvantaged non-nursery group and the difference is found to be beyond the 0·01 level of significance. No significant differences were found between the two advantaged groups on this measure. The results of this analysis are given in Table 4 in the Appendix, page 188.

The Noun Phrase (instance) Index reflects what happens when the child elects to elaborate at the point of the noun phrase in the underlying sentence, but he can also choose to use a pronoun at that point. A reflection of the effect of the choice made with respect to the underlying noun phrase can be gained by using a second index, which takes all the points at which nouns occur, or pronouns are used, as points at which noun phrases might have been elaborated. We refer to this as the Noun Phrase (opportunity) Index, and it is calculated by totalling all the scores for the noun phrases used by the child and finding the mean score for the total number of nouns and pronouns used.

Using this index, the differences between the advantaged groups and the disadvantaged groups is seen to be even greater. The children in the disadvantaged groups more frequently select pronouns for making reference and so the possibilities for elaboration are effectively reduced. The results show that the disadvantaged children relied far more frequently on pronouns for reference than the advantaged groups.

The Use of Pronouns

The use of the pronoun is an interesting feature for study, and is worthy of further consideration at this point since it has figured largely in some other recent studies. We shall return to the methods of analysis used by Courtney Cazden after a short digression in order to look at children's use of pronouns and nouns rather more closely.

At the age of 2 years few children use any pronouns and naming is the rule, but the child's facility to match situations with language increases with the acquisition of the small closed set of pronouns. It is in a way an important triumph in generalisation and relieves him of his dependency for communication on the naming of each item. At the same time it extends the child's practice in matching gesture, rather than in matching the images of objects and actions, with representations through language; it allows him to communicate within the concrete situation using a limited vocabulary.

Since the child's speech in any case at this stage refers more often to the ongoing situation, the fact that he chooses pronouns instead of nouns for representation may not hinder his efforts at communication. The most important consequence may be that by choosing to use the pronoun rather than the noun the opportunity to modify or qualify in some way may be neglected. Thus items of information that refer to attributes of quantity and quality, and which might be expected to appear within the linguistic representations, may not only be less frequent, but it is possible that the child may less frequently become aware of such attributes. On the other hand the child who frequently chooses the noun, when the object

2

referred to is present, not only extends to himself the opportunity to represent attributes, but practises what is in effect a more efficient form of representation for communication when the concrete situation is no longer present to support his intention. He is building habits that will be of advantage to him when he must deal with the world in its absence.

The use of the pronoun has been of some interest in the study of the language of 5-year-olds which has been carried out at the Sociological Research Unit at the Institute of Education, University of London. In the work reported by Hawkins, samples of working-class and middle-class children were seen in an interview, during which they were asked to perform six different tasks, each of which was designed to elicit different kinds of speech and to involve language in a variety of situations (Hawkins, 1969).

The use of the nominal group (that is the means by which reference is made by the use of nouns or pronouns) by these children was examined for differences in complexity. A trend was discovered that pointed to the fact that the middle-class children more frequently chose a noun for making reference, whereas the working-class children tended more frequently to use a pronoun for reference. This led to a further examination of the use of the pronoun.

A paper by Hasan (1968) discusses the concept of reference and cohesion within and between clauses and sentences. Reference can be made forward or backward in the narrative. Pronouns used in this way bring a cohesion to the utterances. Hasan distinguishes three types of reference using pronouns, 'Anaphoric reference' is reference backwards, as in 'The boy kicked *the ball* and *it* broke the window'. 'Cataphoric reference' is forward reference as in '*It* was *the ball* that broke the window'. This second type is far less frequently used by children than the former, according to Hawkins. A third type of reference is known as 'exophoric' and this refers outwards to the context of the situation as in '*It* broke *that*' where there is no information in the child's utterance to identify 'it' or 'that'.

These three categories of reference were applied by Hawkins to two stories produced by the children. The use of cataphoric reference was found to be quite rare, and therefore was included with anaphoric reference. It was found that the use of anaphoric reference differs very little between the middle-class and working-class children in the groups. Exophoric reference, however, was found to be used by the working-class children half as often again as by the middle-class children.

When the children in the Hawkins study were compared on the use of the noun, it was found that the middle-class children more frequently used the noun together with other adjectives and modifying phrases which its use allows. The evidence is that not only do the working-class children use more pronouns, with the consequent loss of related items, but they use more of the exophoric type of reference. Hawkins suggests that it is by this means that middle-class children achieve more specificity and elaboration.

We examined the speech samples of the 3-year-old children in the Language and Environment project in order to discover the extent of anaphoric use and exophoric use of pronouns. It seemed that our use of the Noun Phrase (opportunity) Index might have given a distorted picture as it did not take into account the fact that some pronouns, those used anaphorically, stand for a noun phrase, perhaps an elaborated one, that appears within the same utterance.

The data in the Language and Environment project were much greater for each child than had been the case in the Hawkins study and consequently there appeared larger numbers of instances of pronouns used for exophoric and anaphoric reference. This meant that a comparison based on the numbers of children using each category was not appropriate. In order to have a useful basis for comparison an index of reference for each child and each group is computed by expressing the total number of instances of anaphoric reference as a percentage of the total of both anaphoric and exophoric references. From Table 4 in the Appendix, page 188, it can be seen that when a pronoun is selected for use the children from the advantaged groups are three times as likely to choose it to refer to items already named than are the disadvantaged groups. The difference between the advantaged and disadvantaged groups, on this measure, is found to be statistically highly significant.

Again a difference is also found between the two disadvantaged groups and this is found to be at the $p = 0.01$ level of significance. The disadvantaged nursery group generally have higher scores than the non-nursery disadvantaged group.

The use of exophoric reference, it would seem, leads to a loss of effectiveness in communication. The children in the disadvantaged groups are seen more frequently to use a pronoun without providing any other verbal reference to support it. The use of the pronoun in this way makes great demand on the listener since he must follow the child's actions and focus of attention if he is to understand the intended reference.

From this it would seem that the advantaged groups are regularly practising the use of more specification within the noun phrase than are the members of the disadvantaged groups. The tendency for the disadvantaged groups to use pronouns without other supporting verbal references more frequently is an aspect which seems likely to have important consequences for their effectiveness in communicating with others. Since they are not using explicit reference in ongoing situations, an orientation may be established which will lead to lack of explicitness when communication is more dependent on explicit reference because talk refers away from the ongoing concrete situation.

Verb Complexity

We return now to consider the analysis of the verb phrase; this is based on examining the number of transformations that have been applied in order to realise particular surface structures.

A measure of the complexity of the verb has been attempted before. For example, as early as 1935 Smith had used a count of parts of verbs to show that the proportion of conjugated verbs of all types increased almost three times between the ages of 2 and 5 (Smith, 1935). Bernstein also used a method of counting verbal stems containing more than three units, exclusive of negation, and then expressed this total as a proportion of the total number of finite verbs present in the utterances as a basis for comparison (Bernstein, 1958).

When listening to the speech of young children it is clear that there are several problems associated with the development of the use of the verb. There are the problems of observing the morphological rules, for example, the marking of agreement between subject and predicate in the third person singular. Children also have problems in developing the use of verb auxiliaries that make possible the expression of particular shades of meaning.

In the work referred to earlier, Cazden has extended the ideas of Smith and Bernstein and identified four basic elements which provide the basis for the measurement of the verb (Cazden, 1965). These four elements are: past (e.g. the addition of 'ed'), current relevance ('have' and participle), limited duration ('be' + 'ing') and passive ('be' + participle). These four elements appear in combination, and pairs of modal auxiliaries (e.g. 'could have') allow the expression of conditionality and the sequence of tenses. Points are assigned to each of these elements and to each transformation (e.g. the question transformation). On this basis no verb complex in the Cazden data scored more than four points.

For the present analysis the Cazden system was extended to accommodate the greater variety and complexity in the use of the verb by the children in this sample. The weighting was adjusted at the lower end of the scale to accommodate three items that appear early in the developmental pattern and that are frequently used: these are the imperative unmarked verb form, and the two items 'got' and 'gone'. Auxiliaries that produce the future and conditional tenses were weighted more heavily. Scores were allocated to each element on the basis of complexity of transformation; the score for each verb complex is then the sum of the scores for all elements in the verb complex. Thus the utterance 'You try painting a picture' scores 5 points since the unmarked verb (Vum) scores 2 points and the present participle (Vpr.p) scores 3 points.

The highest score made by any child at the age of 3 in the sample using this scale was 11 points: e.g. 'She might be going to ring someone' =

auxiliary (modal) (4 points)+auxiliary (unmarked) (2 points)+present participle (3 points)+infinitive (2 points). The scale was designed to accommodate even greater complexity than would be found in the talk of 3-year-olds. The system of scoring the verb phrase is given in the Appendix, page 184, together with a list of examples of constructions that were found in the data.

The Verb Complexity Index for each child is calculated by computing the mean score for the verb complexes used. The results of the analysis for each group can be seen in Table 4 in the Appendix. The differences between the advantaged and disadvantaged groups are found to be highly significant and the advantaged groups tend towards greater elaboration of the verb phrase than the disadvantaged groups. The nursery disadvantaged group is again found to produce higher indices than the non-nursery group and in this case the non-nursery advantaged group registered a mean score higher than the advantaged nursery group but not at a level of statistical significance.

The expansion of the verb complex is important because particular meaning can be expressed through it, which leads to more specific information being given about the time sequence, and particularly allows the expression of grades or shades of tentativeness. It would seem that the children in the advantaged groups have already learned to operate over a wider range with the verb complex than have the children in the disadvantaged groups.

Interpreting the Results of the Linguistic Analyses

What can be inferred from the results of the analysis of structural features of the language of the 3-year-olds in the study? First, perhaps, in showing that clear differences exist between the advantaged and disadvantaged groups on all the features that have been examined, we have merely confirmed the link that has already been shown to exist between social class and the child's development of language. We would point out, however, that the link between the two should not be taken as a causal link. The father's occupation is not likely to determine the child's development of language, but rather must it be that all those conditions that have led the father to earn his living by following a particular occupation are likely also to play a part in the kind of environment in which the child will grow up. Such conditions are likely to include the father's social origins, his upbringing and education, his training and qualifications, and the influence of the particular social groups with which he identifies; all these will have exerted their influence on the kind of occupation he will have taken up. The same conditions are also likely to play a part in what goes on in his home: they are likely to influence the kind of woman he will choose to marry and the kind of upbringing which they are then likely to provide for their children.

But the link between social class and the development of language has already been established, in the USA, by Templin (1957), Deutsch (1965) and Strickland (1962) to name but a few. In this country the work of Moore (1967), Sampson (1956) and the work of the Sociological Unit at the London Institute of Education, led by Professor Bernstein, have also established the link.

In the Language and Environment project, however, there would seem to be evidence that differences in the development of language exist even when the measured intelligence of the groups of children at the age of 3 was about the same.

There is also the question of the differences that were found between the two disadvantaged groups. As far as could be seen, these two groups were drawn from similar populations and were of about the same measured intelligence and were generally friendly and outgoing. However, because it was felt that the nursery group should not be recorded until they were settled in school, they had been in the nursery for an average of six weeks at the time of recording. Whilst every effort was made to see that the author was equally familiar to all children it seems likely that the children in the nursery group were already more familiar with the kind of play situation that was set up, and perhaps also, because of their experiences with adults in the nursery, were more familiar with the expectations of adults in the type of play situation used. This seems to be the most likely explanation of the differences between the two disadvantaged groups, but it clearly must be taken into account when the final results are being interpreted.

But how should the general findings from the linguistic analysis of differences between the disadvantaged and advantaged groups of 3-year-olds be interpreted? The differences in the mean length of utterances could be explained by the fact that the disadvantaged children were making fewer transformations in the noun and verb phrases. It was not that there were fewer opportunities at which to apply transformations: the children made reference to both objects and actions, or states, as frequently as the advantaged, but what happened at those points tended to be different. In the case of the noun phrase, the pronoun was selected for reference more frequently, but even when nouns were selected there was less elaboration used than by the advantaged group.

In the case of the verb phrase, the advantaged groups produced larger numbers of higher scoring verb phrases, which means that they were making agreements more regularly, but also that they were using more extensions of the verb. Modals were given a weighted score, but few were used even by the advantaged groups and so this could not of itself account for the large differences in the indices.

Is it possible that the disadvantaged children have learned less about the grammar of their language? Is it that the innate mechanisms proposed by the theory of generative grammar are not so effective as in the advantaged children? Or is it that the children have not met enough experience from which to extract the rules?

Is it that the amount of correction or feedback supplied by the mother is less in the case of the disadvantaged child? This might be partly the case since in the interview the mothers of the advantaged children claimed to play a more positive role in helping the child to 'correct' use although not claiming that they were instructing him in how to use language. Or might it be that the disadvantaged child is indeed exposed to less adult talk than the advantaged child, either because he spends more time out with the peer group away from his mother's influence, or because mothers do not see their role as one of talking with children?

But is it possible that the inferences implied by these questions are unjustified? Does the fact that the children in the disadvantaged groups made lower mean scores on all measures necessarily mean that they had learned less about language, and were less skilled in operating transformations?

If we look at the results of the analysis again we can see that the inferences we are making may not be justified. Although it is clear from Table 2 that the children in the disadvantaged groups used shorter utterances than those in the advantaged groups and that the mean length of the five longest utterances used by children in the disadvantaged groups was less than those of the advantaged groups, it is also clear that at least some of the children in the disadvantaged groups used utterances that were longer than eight words on some occasions. But, for some reason, children in the disadvantaged groups used longer utterances much less frequently than children in the advantaged groups.

From Table 3 we can see that although the total number of complex utterances was four times greater for the advantaged groups than for the disadvantaged groups, nevertheless it is clear that on some occasions some of the children in the disadvantaged groups used complex utterances.

The problem then is not simply that children in the disadvantaged groups are not able to use complex language. Clearly some, if not all, can. What other explanations might there be of the differences that have been shown to exist between these groups of bright talkative 3-year-olds? This became the important issue for the project, and finding other ways of examining the problem became its major concern.

Chapter 4

Language and Meaning

The analyses of the language used by the groups of 3-year-olds in the study indicated that there were differences between the groups in the frequency with which particular structural features occurred. These results support the research findings of others, particularly those of Bernstein and his associates, in showing that there are differences in the forms of language used by children from lower and upper socio-economic groups. From the evidence of the present study, it would seem that these differences are developing by the age of 3.

But what do these differences represent? Are they important except as a marker of social class? Could it not be that these differences are minor differences in surface structure which neither stem from, nor communicate, differences in the complexity of underlying meanings? In seeking to make inferences from the analyses we must look for theories that will offer convincing explanations of how and why such differences come into being and help us to consider whether such differences are likely to affect the child's ability to respond to his experiences in school.

There has been a great deal of research in this area during recent years, but most prominent has been the work of Professor Bernstein and the Sociological Research Unit based at the Institute of Education, London University. Bernstein has brought together sociological, linguistic and psychological considerations to put forward a very persuasive and particularly fruitful theory. This theory has been founded on the work of others, but the views of Luria, Sapir and Whorf have been particularly influential.

Sapir argues that our way of perceiving and understanding the world is conditioned by the language that is available for us to use, that is, our conceptualisation of the 'real world' is unconsciously built upon the language habits of the group of which we are a part (Sapir, 1921).

Whorf's view was based originally on the comparisons he made between the ways in which the language of the Hopi Indians represented aspects of time and space and the devices used in standard European languages. Since the people speaking those languages displayed very different conceptualisations of time and space, Whorf argued that these differences were a direct result of using the different languages. Whorf concluded from his study that fundamental ways of viewing the world are embodied in, and constrained by, language and that there are connections, if not correspondence and correlation, between cultural values, concepts and practices, and linguistic patterns (Whorf, 1941).

Bernstein was amongst the first to recognise that this theory might offer an explanation of the differences that occur between dominant and sub-dominant cultures within a society. In the first place, he set out to investigate the way in which social class is related to educational attainment, and the part that language plays in linking the two.

In an early paper, Bernstein claims that

... social structure transforms language possibilities into a specific code which elicits, reinforces and generalises distinct types of relationships with the environment and this creates particular dimensions of significance. (Bernstein, 1961, p. 288)

In the development of the theory that has taken place since then, the view that language creates particular dimensions of significance has remained an unaltered basic underlying principle. Bernstein conceives language as functioning within social classes to provide the means by which class 'subcultures' can reproduce themselves. Different social structures, then, are likely to produce different ways of using language and this, in turn, is likely to affect the kinds of meanings that different groups attach to their everyday experiences.

For example, the possibilities that the middle class recognise for maintaining or improving their material possessions and social position, through education and occupation, lead to long-term planning, and immediate pleasures and rewards may be sacrificed in order to work for greater achievement some time in the future. In families where it is known that ambitions cannot be realised immediately and where deliberate planning makes clear the recognition of cause–effect relationships, the existence of a rational basis for behaviour must be communicated to members of the family. Explanations of this approach to life indicate the kind of structure that must be placed upon experiences. The need for motives and values to be understood by the children leads to the expression of feelings, and so to empathy, and the appeal for understanding is directed to the individual. Thus, explicitness is essential, for the basis of understanding is, as it were, a theoretical approach to problems, and an examination of general principles and possible alternative interpretations and consequences that might arise from different courses of action and behaviour.

But the lower working class accept the restricted range of occupations open to them; work is the reality over which they have little control; they see little choice and prospect of change, so their hopes and ambitions are inevitably limited. Work is generally, for the lower working class, a routine that requires no planning on their part. The bond which they share is the work they do, and conditions of work, and people's roles, are established by tradition.

In such circumstances, there is little to provoke the use of language for discrimination and planning, but it is more likely to serve to establish and maintain common interests and solidarity. There may be little gained for the lower working class by analysis and discrimination, and good relationships are likely to be maintained most readily by recognising the position of members in the group. It is not essential for language that is used for such purposes to be explicit, for if meanings are shared, communication can go on through highly predictable short phrases, and idiomatic sequences can be used to refer to commonly shared experiences. In the family where parents maintain such a view of life, the child has a particular role, that of child, or boy or girl, assigned to him and he is helped to recognise the status of each member of the family.

It is the expectations and aspirations of people that are different and it is these differences that lead to different views of relationships with others. The way in which language is used by parents and others in the home and the part the child is expected to play determine the kind of experiences in using language he will meet. Much of the child's early learning, then, both about using language and about ways of behaving, and about the world around, results from the way in which people, particularly his mother, talk with him.

Bernstein suggests, therefore, that, as children are brought up in such different environments and are exposed to different attitudes and values and to different outlooks on the world in general, they are not only developing different ways of viewing the world but they are also building up different orientations towards the use of language, which reflect differences in the organisation of the *meaning* of their experiences.

The term 'code' is now well known, although there may be some misunderstandings about what the term refers to. Bernstein adopted the terms 'restricted' and 'elaborated' codes and originally illustrated the differences between the two in terms of the characteristic uses of linguistic structures. Thus, he contrasted the short, simple utterances of those who operate a 'restricted code' with the elaborated and complex utterances of those who operate an 'elaborated' code.

This part of Bernstein's theory has met with considerable criticism and it has been taken to mean that he is in fact concerned with styles of speaking and not so much with the kind of meanings which are being expressed. In a recent paper (Bernstein, 1973a, p. 70), he insists that he has never been concerned with the differences between social groups at the level of 'competence' but has always been concerned with differences in 'performance': that is, not with inner knowledge of language, but with what people say. He also insists that he has never suggested that working-class children were lacking in their basic tacit understanding of the linguistic rule system, but that he has concerned himself with the sociological controls in the use to which this common understanding has been put. Again, he has stated that because a code is 'restricted' it does not follow that the children cannot ever produce elaborated speech, but it does mean that when such speech is used it will be in specific situations. The theory, as it has developed, has become more and more complex in order to account for a number of different orientations within families that will influence the child.

There have been many criticisms of Bernstein's work, most notably by William Labov, who, in quoting the speech samples he obtained from two black American youths, aims to show that it is possible to conduct logical argument in non-standard English and that the use of standard English does not, of itself, generate rationality (Labov, 1970).

It is clear from the arguments that Bernstein and his team have put forward that they are claiming that differences in the incidence of particular structural features displayed in the talk of children from different social classes *are* a reflection of different *meanings*, and of differences in the orientation of children towards the use of language (Bernstein, 1971). We shall return to discuss the relationships between linguistic structures and meanings in a later chapter, but first we shall consider how the hypotheses, implicit in the work of Bernstein and his associates, that children develop different orientations to the use of language, and establish different meanings, might be tested.

What is *meaning* and how can differences in the meanings available to children be examined? How can differences in the orientation to use language be identified and measured?

What Is Meaning?

There is no problem in finding answers to the question 'What is language?': all writers are likely to indicate that language is a system of signs through which those who know the system can transmit meanings; language is a medium for the expression and reception of meanings. But when the question 'What is meaning?' is asked, answers are likely to be less direct and lead into philosophical discussions of the problems of defining meaning. Yet whatever we do, whatever we say, indicates that we are always operating on a basis of meanings: meaning exists, even though its definition is elusive.

We tend, however, to think of 'meaning' mainly in relation to words. When we define what a word means, we offer alternatives, words or phrases that can be substituted for the words in question. Once language has been acquired, it becomes the vehicle for carrying meaning, not only for communication with others, but as a means of communicating with ourselves, that is, it allows us to reflect on meanings.

If we ask how children develop language, however, we are likely to find answers that refer to the development of the structures of language.

Recent developments of transformational grammar, as we have seen in Chapter 2, have provided a theoretical framework that offers a way of explaining the sequence in which the structures of language gradually emerge. There is no doubt either that the study of language through the framework of transformational grammar throws up problems of meaning and of derivational complexity. But the problems of meaning tend to be those that illuminate the underlying differences in derivation that account for differences in meaning when surface structure appears to be similar.

The concept of 'deep structure' is clearly concerned with meaning, although it does not seem that the term refers to the underlying meaning of 'kernel' sentences (referred to in Chapter 2). The term 'deep structure' as used by Chomsky and others seems to refer to the 'innate' organising mechanisms that differentiate aspects of meaning into the basic components to form kernel sentences (Chomsky, 1965).

'Deep structure' would seem to refer to the capacity of human beings to differentiate objects from the actions through which objects are related, and to recognise the temporal sequencing of events when the 'actor' initiates action that consequently relates to the 'acted upon'. This innate ability of man to classify the different components of his experiencing seems to be based on physical and psychological universals that relate to the organisation of perceptions. That transformational grammar 'works', that is, that the observed facts fit the propositions of transformational grammar well, seems likely to be so, not because the child has under his control linguistic formulae, but rather because linguistic formulae have emerged because of man's innate capabilities for processing perceptions and articulating sounds, both of which provide constraints within which language must develop. The characteristics imposed by these constraints would seem to shape all languages and therefore could be considered to be the 'universals' of language. However, whatever it is that is 'innate', it would seem that 'deep structure' is not itself the underlying meaning but the framework through which meanings can be organised.

But how do meanings arise? For the newborn child there is, perhaps, nothing that could with justification be called meaning: he alternates between states of comfort and discomfort. But with the passing weeks and months we can observe the meanings that different situations are beginning to have for him. He focuses his eyes upon his bottle or feeding cup and the meaning it has for him is demonstrated by his response. We can see pleasure and urgency combined in his face, in his heightened activity and in the change in tension as he begins to take food. Both object and situation clearly have meaning for him: meaning seems to be both the expectation and the realisation of the feeding situation. Yet it is not likely at this point that there is an 'awareness' of meaning: the child is not able yet to contemplate the meaning. He experiences a state of hunger and associates food with the experiences that come as that state is reduced.

Only much later will the child recognise the meaning of the state of hunger and begin to look for food, and it will be much later again before he recognises the state for what it is and says 'I'm hungry'.

In the meantime, 'meaning' is more and more being attached to objects and actions and to situations, as the child builds up anticipation of the response he will make. 'Meaning', then, seems to begin with the differentiation of experiences; for example, the recognition of pattern in events, and the recognition of obstructions that break familiar sequences and that perhaps begin to build up an awareness of expectations. The sound of approaching footsteps becomes associated with the appearance of the parent, the sound of a familiar voice, and lifting. The baby quietens his cries in expectation of the familiar routine. When the familiar does not happen, there is a renewed protest, a recognition, perhaps, that expectations have not been fulfilled.

Gradually, then, the child begins to recognise structure in his experiences. He is lifted on to the adult's knee, and anticipates rocking or tossing movements that he has experienced before. If this does not immediately happen, he begins to rock or toss himself, trying to enact his own part in the familiar situation, and reproducing the effects of the actions of the adult and so, with intention, he communicates his wishes to the adult.

Meaning lies in the situation, then, in what he has learned to associate, to anticipate and expect. But anticipation and expectation now begin to play a part, and the meaning is imposed on the situation by the child himself. So meaning lies in the situation and in the anticipation of his own part in the situation, and in his own framework of expectations through which he will view the situation.

Thus, before language develops, meanings are becoming differentiated and meanings are being imposed on situations.

In considering the meaning of meaning, Ogden and Richards (1923) recognise a number of different categories of meaning, for example, meaning can relate to intention, purpose or function, or to emotive meaning, that is, to feelings and attitudes, or to referential meaning, that is, to reference made within a context.

Words act as gestures made towards others and the meaning that is attached to them stems from the behaviour that can be observed to follow from it.

Meaning arises and lies within the field of the relation between the gesture of a given human organism and the subsequent behaviour of this organism as indicated to another human organism by that gesture. (Mead (1934), 1964, p. 163)

Thus Mead considers the way in which words come to have meaning. The child observes 'words' being used and the meaning that he attaches to them relates to the situations in which they appear and the behaviour of the speaker as he uses words. 'It is the social process,' says Mead, 'which relates the responses of one individual to the gestures of another as the meaning of the latter' (p. 165).

The child's language arises out of situations that have come to have meaning for him and the production of holophrases is the first evidence that uttered sounds carry intentions of different kinds. Halliday refers to these different intentions and relates them to the functions they serve. The response of the listener to the holophrasic speech of the child is important in helping the child to elaborate his utterances and lead him towards the structures of language (Halliday, 1973).

'Holophrases' are in many ways the creation of the child alone, although the adult helps to shape and differentiate the utterances as he responds to the child. But after the 'holophrases', words are not then something that the child creates for himself, they are part of the situation that surrounds him and cannot be separated from it. The words he learns and the linguistic structures that become available to him are those of a particular language which is itself the instrument of the particular culture.

Even while he is still learning to operate the system, language itself begins to shape meaning for him, as it is used to help him adapt his behaviour to become an acceptable member of the family, and also to accept the values and expectations of the wider society.

To what extent does the language we *experience*, as used by others, and the *employment* of language itself affect the meaning that experience can have for us? We have, in an earlier chapter, shown how classification is aided by the use of words, and how, by indicating what something is *not*, the child is helped to see what to include or not include within a particular class. Thus, a variety of dogs, from tiny toy dogs to the Great Dane, will be included in the class 'dog', thereby implicitly directing the child's attention to what aspects are 'dog-like', and other animals that may have features that are similar – fur, four legs – are excluded by other criteria. The use, too, of class terms, for example 'furniture' and 'clothes', helps the child to put a clearer structure upon things that are used for similar purposes. Roger Brown has referred to the ways in which the child learns to put a structure on the world around him as 'the Original Word Game'; and so it must be that the very naming of the components of the world and the classification which 'concept' terms offer help the child to extract principles and order the elements of his experience (Roger Brown, 1958). More than that, the very naming of situations like 'party' or 'school' or 'home', or activities like 'shopping' or 'cleaning' or 'playing', embraces objects, actions and activities that set structure upon complex situations that involve people, actions, objects and the relationships between them. This helps the child to classify and place some order on day-by-day activities in the home and neighbourhood.

But language used by others as they talk with the child perhaps does more than this. It helps the child to develop those concepts that might be seen to be 'ambiguous' and not easily delineated. Some notions would seem to be developed easily and without the help of language: for example, the child may learn that the table is 'hard' by banging his head and then learn to avoid a repetition; or learn that the teapot is hot, without necessarily having a word to label the qualities. But once the words 'hot' and 'hard' are understood, it becomes possible to help him avoid pain by forewarning him about other situations which are likely to prove painful.

Vygotsky's classical experiment indicates the role that naming attributes plays in delineating concepts. A set of twenty-two blocks was used, that was formed of different combinations of colour, shape, height and size and had four nonsense words written on the underside of the blocks. These terms disregarded colour and shape and distinguished large tall figures, small tall figures, flat large figures and flat small figures. The experiment shows the increased rapidity with which the child is able to place order on any or all of the blocks once he begins to recognise the attributes to which the terms refer. The experimenters conclude that concept formation cannot be reduced

to association, attention, imagery, inference or determining. They are all indispensable, but they are insufficient without the use of the sign or word or the means by which we direct our mental operations, control their course and channel them towards the solution of the problem confronting us. (Vygotsky (1934), 1962, p. 59)

Vygotsky concludes:

Learning to direct one's own inventive processes with the aid of words or signs is an integral part of the process of concept formation, although this kind of activity is seen to be one which does not come to the fore until adolescence. (Ibid., p. 59)

Concepts are seen as being formed by intellectual operations in which words first direct attention to the relevant attributes and make possible the abstraction of relevant attributes and then lead to synthesising, as others offer words which 'hold' these complex meanings.

We can see that the experiences which children have of adults using language with them must play an important part in influencing the kind of interpretation that children will make of their everyday experiences. The priorities that adults have in using language with children, what they choose to express in language, serves to direct the child's attention to particular features of his experiences. If, for example, the adult is talking about particular detail in the environment, the structure of plants, the shape and colour of the rainbow, the reflections in puddles, then the child's attention is being drawn to aspects that he might not have noticed had no one spoken with him about them, or, if he had, might have remained at a level of interpretation that did not require conscious awareness of detail, and reflection on the nature of the phenomenon.

That the use of words can make a difference to the way in which the child will respond to the non-dominant aspects of the world around him has been demonstrated effectively in a series of experiments by Luria.

In some of these experiments Luria shows how the words the child uses to instruct himself bring his own action more closely under his control. Children responding to a panel of lights, for example, were found to be bringing their actions under much greater control by 'talking' to themselves and verbalising instructions to themselves (Luria, 1959).

A later experiment showed that putting a verbal interpretation on an experience could make a non-dominant aspect stand out as clearly as a dominant one. For example, when the child was responding to pictures of aeroplanes on different coloured backgrounds, he naturally gave closer attention to the aeroplane than to the background, but when attention was drawn to the background by explaining, for example, that 'when the sky is yellow, that means it's sunny and the aeroplane can fly', the child was able to respond to the background and to see it as an important feature of the picture, so much so that it governed the interpretation that he made (Luria, 1961).

The language of others, then, directs the child's attention so that he begins to take the perspective of those who talk with him. Where values are expressed, the child begins to attach importance to those aspects valued by the adults, and begins to structure his own perceptions differently, putting a different interpretation upon what he sees or hears.

Luria puts forward the examples of twins to illustrate the changes that are brought about as a direct result of the development of language (Luria and Yudovitch, 1959). The twins were seriously retarded in the development of language and their play was consequently repetitive and unstructured and unplanned. In the experiment the twins were separated in the nursery school so that they were motivated to interact more with other people. The more retarded of the two was given special attention, including the fostering of language.

After ten months, the general improvement in intellectual functioning in both boys was most marked, but the twin who had received special speech experiences was markedly ahead of his brother, although previously he had been considered the more retarded of the two. This child now used speech for planning, and also for narrative, more frequently than his brother and the difference was most prominent where imagination and the anticipation of events were required. He also demonstrated greater control of grammar, and so showed greater differentiation of meaning, through developed, extended utterances.

Equally important, this twin who, in the first place, was the more passive of the two, now began to take on leadership and direct the play of others. He told stories readily when asked and when responding to pictures was able to interpret the scene as a whole, as though it illustrated some story. His brother, on the other hand, was less confident in telling stories and responded to pictures by giving an inventory of the items in the picture without attempting to relate them and put them into a structured whole interpretation.

The differences in the approach to their experiences seemed to be in the meaningfulness of what was perceived, that is, in the interpretation that the child could place on the events he was meeting: the world around now seemed to take on a meaning that was different for each twin. But the help with language that had been given to the second twin did not seem to consist of a very elaborate treatment. We are told that the child was first helped actively to name objects and then actively to answer questions, to describe pictures and explain his activities. In other words, he was given experiences of interaction with adults that we would expect many children to have with their parents.

But above all, perhaps, the language others are using reveals the kind of value that they set upon aspects of their experiences and upon the worth of other people and the attitudes they take up towards other people. The child's view of other people and his awareness of their needs, the kind of relationships he expects to enter into with other people, as well as the view he takes of himself, are all influenced by, and may be dependent upon, the views expressed by those around him. Through the talk of others he learns to place significance upon particular aspects and relationships. What gains priority for his attention, and for communicating to others, is likely to be the consequence of what has been communicated to him through the talk of others.

What kind of meanings do children place on their everyday experiences? Is it the case that meanings are developing differently and that children will make interpretations of experiences that are consistently different from those made by others? And how should we recognise that there are differences between children in the meanings they would place on similar experiences?

From the foregoing discussion it would seem that differences in meaning would be reflected in the differences in the responses that children make to the same situation. Differences in meaning are likely to be reflected in the way in which children respond by using language, and an examination of the use of language may indicate, not only what they have learned about using language, but also the kind of interpretation they are disposed to set on their experiences.

Although meaning clearly resides within the child, it is only through the outward evidence of his response, through his general behaviour and his use of language, that we are able to infer what 'meaning' is for him.

The young child's use of language, then, is a major indication of the range of inner meanings that are governing his responses. An examination of the purposes for which language is used may be the most appropriate basis on which to compare the meanings which are available to young children. The speech data collected at the age of 3, in similar play situations, offered evidence of the meanings that governed the children's responses as they played with their chosen friends. The data offered an opportunity for looking at the functions that the children's language fulfilled and for considering whether there were differences in the way in which children drew on these functions as a means of realising the meanings that governed their responses to the play context.

Chapter 5

A Classification of the Uses of Language

As we considered the inferences that might be drawn from the analyses of the structural features in the language produced by children, we reflected on our purposes in analysing the collected data. We saw our task to be that of trying to discover the kind of meanings that children were establishing, and of testing whether there were differences between children in the systems of meanings which were developing that might stem from differences in their experiences of using language.

Our interest lay, therefore, in the way in which language functioned to express and construct different kinds of meanings, meanings that would reflect the child's awareness, appreciation and interpretation of the physical and social world around him.

We were concerned, then, to examine the functions that language serves, and we looked to theories and research that would guide us in setting up a classification on which a functional analysis of children's language could be based. This is an area that has interest for linguists, sociologists and psychologists and a number of different frameworks for an analysis of the functions of language have been proposed. Recently Peter Robinson has examined the literature that provides a background to the study of the functions of language (Robinson, 1972), and as a social-psychologist he found the framework put forward by Jacobson to be the one that offered the most fruitful basis for analysis (Jacobson, 1960). We also had considered this framework for the purpose of classifying the recorded talk of the 3-year-olds in our study. In practice we found that the functions making up this framework, that is the *emotive*, the *conative*, the *referential*, the *poetic*, the *phatic* and the *metalingual*, left much of the children's language undifferentiated within broad categories, which were recognised by the linguistic forms of utterances.

A classification set out by Firth (cited by Hymes, 1964), which is based on the forms of speech that can be ascribed to particular roles that are played in a range of social contexts, also focused on linguistic structure and so seemed unlikely to help us.

We have already referred to Michael Halliday's work, and we turned to the framework that he sets out (Halliday, 1973). The uses of language which make up this classification, that is, the *instrumental*, the *regulative*, the *interactional*, the *heuristic*, the *imaginative* and the *representational* or *informative*, can be seen to occur in children's talk. But, in practice, the classification did not differentiate large sections of the children's talk. Many of their utterances would, for example, have fallen within the category *informative* but there are great differences in the kinds of meanings that can be included in the category described as *informative*, and it was important that these should be distinguished.

Halliday's own view is that once the child has acquired grammatical structures he draws on formal linguistic features to express particular meanings (Halliday, 1973). His classification has been designed, therefore, to provide a framework for studying language, and for considering the potential for expressing meaning that particular structures hold. The problem is that we cannot assume that children deliberately select and employ structures with the intention of realising the potential meaning of the structures. When children use language we frequently see that they employ particular features in such a way that it is clear they have not yet discovered the agreed or assigned meanings. The young child's use of 'because' may be taken as an example. Even though the child uses the word frequently it does not necessarily mean that he is aware of, and is referring to, a causal relationship. The child's use of 'because' results often in elliptical arguments which take the form 'It's so because it is' or 'You must because you must'.

Theoretical models which are useful to the linguist do not necessarily provide suitable models upon which to analyse the functions of children's language. The linguist's view of *function* is one that relates to the language itself, whilst the question that we are raising is how language functions in the development of meaning.

Piaget's Contribution

We turned then to consider Piaget's contribution to the study of children's language. This work is well known and has been used as a model for many years. His classification of language arose from his essential concern with the characteristics of children's thinking: his aim was to show how children's thinking is different from adult thought. Language, for Piaget, is the vehicle through which aspects of the child's thinking are revealed and, together with the child's actions, provides the medium through which the child's thinking can be studied.

The central concept which explains the peculiarities of children's thinking is *egocentrism*. It was through the analysis of the language of two 6-year-old children that Piaget arrived at what, for him, were the main distinctive categories of children's talk, that is, he recognised *egocentric* and *socialised* speech (Piaget, 1923). In analysing the talk of these children, Piaget discovered the importance of that talk which he refers to as *egocentric monologue*. This is a sort of running commentary aimed at no audience in particular which is often *sotto voce,* a monotone half with-drawn from the ears of others. Even in what appeared to be socialised speech Piaget found evidence of egocentrism, in that the child showed his inability to conceive the world from any viewpoint but his own.

Socialised speech, according to Piaget, forms the other large section of the child's talk, and embraces a number of different uses of language, all of which are directed towards a listener. Socialised speech includes: demands, requests, questions, answers, criticisms, and a section described as *adapted information,* that is, information expressed in ways that take account of the listener's needs.

This framework clearly offered us a possible basis for the classification of the 3-year-olds' speech, but there were many problems in using the classification. The category egocentric monologue, for example, covers a range of children's use of language in which there are wide differences in the kinds of meaning expressed, as illustrated by the following examples:*

1 *Jill*: There ... baby ... go to sleep now. Another time ... to play ... your mummy's going away ... going ... now ... away ... down the street ... down ... don't cry ... don't cry.

Jill seems quite oblivious to others, whilst she manipulates the doll her voice is low and on a monotone.

2 *Jimmie*: Push it in ... now into there ... brrr round and round ... brr ... it's coming down ... faster ... into there ... brrm ... I'm sending it in there.

Jimmie is pushing a car round the floor. His voice is low, but he makes loud car noises. He does not look up when Tom pushes past him.

3 *John*: Well I'm going to get a big bicycle and it'll have little wheels at the side first ... and then ... and then I'll ride it fast ... and they're off ... off down the road fast. And I'm going to get ... a red one ... I am ... when I'm five.

John speaks directly to Mark but then his attention to Mark fades and his voice falls and he seems unaware that Mark has gone over to the table. He looks up and raises his voice looking in Mark's direction.

4 *Pam*: When this goes running the big lorry goes round.

Pam and Sue are playing alongside each

* The transcriptions which are used throughout the book are punctuated only to show pauses. The mark ... indicates a pause or hesitation, while a full stop indicates a more positive break.

Sue:	Don't go there.	
	That one in bed now.	
Pam:	Watch it go.	
Sue:	Look it's opened its eyes now.	
Pam:	It's going across now.	
	I'm putting bricks on.	
Sue:	It's a little one now.	
Pam:	Tips it up . . . get much out.	

other. They look up at each other now and again but their play and talk are quite separate.

The above are short extracts from longer occurrences of the kind of talk which Piaget refers to as egocentric monologue. Clearly, the talk is for the self. But to classify all these examples as *monologue* has in fact ignored differences in the meanings expressed. Monologue accounts only for the direction in which speech is addressed, and whilst this is of great significance in the child's development, a classification on this basis will not tell us what the child is inclined to talk to himself about – that is, what kinds of meaning gain priority.

There are indeed differences in the kinds of meaning expressed in these monologues. Jill is absorbed in imaginative role play, whilst Jimmie's comments parallel his actions almost as though he is monitoring his own activity, keeping himself aware of his own actions.

John, on the other hand, is projecting through the imagination into the future, anticipating the day he will get a new bicycle.

Sue and Pam are playing together apparently with some awareness of the presence of the other, but each follows her own activity and talks for herself alone: here are monologues in parallel. Pam seems to be monitoring her actions, perhaps at times directing complex action which needs to be precise. Sue is busy playing and perhaps assumes the roles of mother and baby in turn.

The collected talk of 3-year-olds supports Piaget's view that often when the young child talks he forms his own audience. He is unaware of others, even though they may be very near, and his talk is displaying something of the meaning that the play has for him. Often, even though the talk seems to be directed at another person, there is no real awareness of the other person's part in the communication, as is perhaps illustrated in the following example:

Sam: And I can do it properly. I can – better than Brian and I'm first to do it. You see I will.

There is no preceding clue to the listener about the subject of this statement. Sam seems to be trying to prove his superiority and he addresses the adult as though she knows what he is thinking about.

This last example of talk seems to have a different purpose from the other examples, although it would still seem to have the characteristics of egocentrism. Sam seems to be looking for some acknowledgement of his worth, drawing the other's attention to himself and *maintaining the self* through his talk. This kind of talk seems concerned with the way in which the child sees himself in relation to others.

Although all the above examples would seem to fall within Piaget's category of egocentric speech, to class them all as the same neglects important differences in the ideas that are being developed through monologue, that is, in the kinds of meanings which the child finds important to express to himself. Analysis of egocentric monologue might then reveal differences between children in the kinds of meanings that they are disposed to express as they talk to themselves.

Again, if we look at the categories of children's language which are included in socialised speech, there are problems in applying the classification, for the distinctions seem to be dependent on analysing the form of the utterance, that is, relying on structural features for classifying utterances.

For example, the difference between *demand* and *request* is likely to be judged on the basis of the *linguistic structure* of the utterance and the purposes for which the child seeks to influence the adult are ignored, that is, other aspects of meaning are not taken into account. Then again, Piaget's terms *question* and *answer* are part of his classification, but these terms indicate only the part played by those utterances in the interaction and do not refer either to the purpose of questions or to the intentions of answers.

Piaget's classification also recognises an important class of utterances within socialised speech that is referred to as *adapted information*. This term appears to cover those uses of language where elaboration is needed in order for the listener to have an understanding of the meaning which the speaker intends to convey. There are many instances in the data from the 3-year-olds that would be included in the classification as adapted information and yet they illustrate a wide range of meanings that would not be distinguished unless the classification were extended. All the following, for example, would be classified as adapted information:

1   *Sue:*   We got a little dolly and it's very small
and it's got hair like this (she gestures) –
curly.

2   *Mark*:   If you want to get to the moon . . . well . . . you've
to get in a rocket . . . and you've to have something
on you head . . . on the moon.

3   *Tim*:   It doesn't matter if it all burns up if no one wants it any
more.

4   *Jill*:   We might get a cat one day . . . but I think we'll get a
hamster first . . . if my mummy says we can.

There are clearly considerable differences in the degree of 'adaptedness' in these utterances and there are also differences in the kind of information represented.

Sue identifies and gives some detail about a possession, her doll. Mark is making clear a relationship between equipment and the possibilities of space travel. Tim recognises a condition that makes a generally unacceptable act acceptable, and Jill talks about possibilities in the future.

Piaget's classification, however, takes us some way towards a framework, within which the functions of children's language might be analysed. It recognises both social and cognitive functions and differentiates to some extent within these, but it does not provide us with a classification that deals satisfactorily with all the questions with which we are concerned. In later work, Piaget has stressed the importance of the cognitive aspects of language, arguing that it frees communication from the ongoing present concrete situation, and allows the user to escape from the limits of time and space. Language permits the representation in the present of events that are past, or remote, or that never have, and perhaps never will, happen. Language is the vehicle *par excellence* of symbolisation, according to Piaget, permitting the user to represent any aspect of human experience and any known aspect of physical phenomena, so that it can be referred to and examined in its absence (Inhelder and Piaget, 1964).

Piaget clearly recognises, then, the role of language in organising the meaning of experiences, that is in the interpretation the child makes of the world outside the self, and his writings indicate the wide range of notions, or ideas, that language must serve to construct and express.

It was clear from an examination of Piaget's theory that a classification could be developed that would differentiate a greater range of differences in the meanings expressed in language by young children. A consideration of the theoretical viewpoint of others, including the major contributions of Vygotsky, Luria, Lewis, Bruner and Bernstein, led us to set up the classification that is described and discussed in the following pages.

The Functions of Language

The term *function* is defined as the means by which a purpose is achieved. The purpose that language serves in the child's development we see as that of expressing and constructing meanings, that is, language functions in relation to the child's developing conceptualisation of the world around him.

We distinguish, then, four functions that can be recognised by the characteristics of four different modes of thinking that language serves to express and, in our view, promote. The distinctions we recognise are based on, or supported by, well-known research and theories. The following are the functions on which the classification is based. This is a revision of the framework outlined in an earlier paper (Tough, 1973b). This revision does not change the classification on which the analysis of the language of 3-year-olds was based, but reconsiders the distinction between the *functions* and the *uses* of language, and seeks to clarify the notion, and the role, of what we refer to as strategies.

1 THE DIRECTIVE FUNCTION

The directive function is concerned with directing action and operations. At the simplest level it is a running commentary on actions as they are performed, at the most complex it is concerned with the actions of others, and with the actions of the self and others, in planning and co-operating in a sequence of actions or operations.

2 THE INTERPRETATIVE FUNCTION

All language can be said to be concerned with interpretation in some way, but we use the term 'interpretative' in contrast to the term 'directive'. The directive function is concerned with directing actions, the interpretative function is concerned with communicating the meaning of events and situations that, as it were, the child witnesses. Language serves to make an interpretation of, or impose an interpretation on, what the child perceives happening around him. This function is essentially concerned with ongoing experiences, or the memories of past experiences.

3 THE PROJECTIVE FUNCTION

Although all thinking, all meaning, must in the end be based on experiences of some kind, nevertheless the child is capable of thinking that is not tied to the immediate experience, or to remembering past experiences. Thinking can make leaps in time and space, and can be attempts to sample, as it were, the experiences of other people. This kind of thinking seems to depend on drawing upon the imagination and using elements of known experience, to *project* and explore situations in which one is not at the time actually, and may not ever be, taking part. We refer to this as the projective function.

4 THE RELATIONAL FUNCTION

This function is the one with which much recent work has been concerned. Language is seen to play an important role in establishing and maintaining relationships between people. Explicitly or implicitly language plays a part in communicating the relationships that exist between people: language is used to convey the position that the individual assumes towards others.

The General Framework

These then were the four functions of language that it seemed might be in evidence as the child played and talked with his chosen companion. We shall put forward our justifications for recognising these in the general framework for a classification as we discuss each function and differentiate further within each.

Before doing this, however, there are several points that should be made about the general framework.

It was clear that the 3-year-olds in the study produced talk that was not directed towards a listener and to which they were not expecting any response. A good deal of the child's talk seemed to be for himself alone. It was more difficult to decide what part of the child's talk could be described as egocentric, that is, failing to take account of another's viewpoint. Much of the 3-year-old's talk could be expected to reflect the young child's problems of understanding, but setting up criteria by which judgements could be made reliably proved difficult. We were more concerned with the kinds of meanings that the child was attempting to convey, whether to himself or to others. In the end the classification took account only of the direction of the child's talk, that is, whether he addressed his utterances to a listener or not.

We must also make the point that we are not suggesting that each of the child's utterances can be seen to serve one function, and one function only. Most utterances, perhaps, express in some way the kind of relationship in which the speaker holds the person he addresses, but at the same time he may be conveying other kinds of meaning, those that might be considered to reflect his cognitive appraisal of his experiences. Utterances, indeed, reveal that language serves more than one function at the same time.

We distinguished between the relational function and the other three, that is the directive, the interpretative and the projective functions, which we refer to as the *ideational functions*, for reasons that have already been suggested and that will be made clear as we proceed.

Before discussing the ideational and relational functions in more detail, however, we should perhaps make clear the basis on which the classification within functions is made.

If the functions of language are concerned with different kinds of meaning, or thinking, the means by which this will be made evident is through different uses of language. Within each function then different uses of language will be recognised: for example, there appear to be two uses of language within the interpretative function. The first use of language we have described as *reporting*, where elements of the scene are distinguished and perhaps are set within a framework that takes account of several elements. The second use of language that reveals the interpretative function we refer to as *reasoning* in which causal relationships are made explicit, and justifications may be given.

But within the particular uses of language there is need for further differentiation to take account of the different devices that may be used. For example, within the reporting use there may be instances of comparisons, reference to detail, reference to sequence, and a number of other devices which together aid explicitness. We refer to these as *strategies* and distinguish a number that may also serve the several different uses that are distinguished within the functions. The classification, and subsequent analysis, then takes account of the *function*, the *use of language* and the *strategies* employed.

We hope that the points made above will help the reader to follow our description and discussion of the classification which follows.

THE DIRECTIVE FUNCTION

There is considerable support, both from theory and research, for the view that language serves the synpractic or directive function, and the characteristics of language that emerge to serve this function can readily be identified in the talk of the 3-year-olds, from descriptions given by Piaget (1923), Vygotsky (1934), Lewis (1951) and Luria (1959, 1961).

Two uses of language that emerge in the realisation of this function can be recognised: they are language that clearly is *self-directing* and that which is *other-directing*. These uses are essentially concerned with the organisation and implementation of physical actions and operations.

THE SELF-DIRECTING USE OF LANGUAGE

Prominent in the self-directing use of language is talk that is *monitoring* the child's own actions. This is the running commentary, or monologue, to which Piaget (1923) refers, and it seems to keep the child aware of the actions he is performing. Monitoring might be regarded as a strategy through which actions are controlled and directed. Much of the talk in the collected data illustrates strategies of this kind. Language is frequently an accompaniment to the child's actions, as in the following example.

Jimmie: This car goes down here . . . the little car.
Pushing it down here . . . the little car.
All down here . . . pushing it down here . . .
pushing it down here . . la . . la . . . la.

Lewis, in discussing the functions of language, sees this kind of use of language as more than an accompaniment to actions. It is part of the action, and thus the action is a total activity that is both non-linguistic and linguistic (Lewis, 1951). Vygotsky also used the term 'synpratic' to indicate that as well as accompanying action its function is to contribute to, and promote, activity. 'It serves mental orientation, conscious understanding – it helps to overcome difficulties' (Vygotsky, 1962, p. 133).

Sometimes, as in the last example, the child seems to become aware of the quality of the sound he is making, and at a point, marked by a change in the intonation of what he is saying, his talk takes on a song-like quality. Jimmie, in fact, puts both tune and rhythm to the words.

Vygotsky has contributed a great deal to our understanding of the directive function of language. Although his work, which was carried out in Russia before 1934, was not available in English until 1962, it has had considerable influence on studies of language. Vygotsky replicated the situations in which Piaget had collected his data, adding a series of obstructions so that the child was continually faced with frustration. For example, the child perhaps found no pages to draw on, broken pencils and no suitable colours. Under such conditions Vygotsky found that the amount of egocentric speech used by 6-year-olds almost doubled in comparison with those children who did not face such problems.

Vygotsky concluded from this that an impediment, which breaks the flow of the child's intended activity, rouses the child to a new awareness of his own activity, and that his speech expresses that process of becoming aware. But speech serves to provide more than just the refocusing of attention, according to Vygotsky:

Our findings indicate that egocentric speech does not long remain a mere accompaniment to the child's activity. Besides being a means of expression and of release of tension, it soon becomes an instrument in the proper sense – in seeking and planning the solution of the problem. (Vygotsky (1934), 1962, p. 16)

The following examples perhaps are an illustration of this development.

Linda: Putting her to bed.   Linda talks quietly
In the bed. Like that.   to herself. Her voice is almost
Puts legs down.   a monotone. She puts the doll
Now . . .   into the bed – and looks round.

At this point there is a change. 'Now' goes with the previous talk and has the same low tone of voice, but perhaps because she does not see what she needs or expects, an observable change in manner and tone of voice takes place.

Linda: . . . well . . . a cover.   Linda speaks loudly and
Where's a cover?   more clearly, but is not
I'll have to find a cover . . . in   addressing anyone. Her
the box . . . here . . . *that'll*   speech just anticipates

do for a cover . . . there . . .	her action as she turns
put it round . . . make you warm . . .	to the box and turns over
There . . . that's nice and warm baby.	the contents. She returns
	to the bed, and gradually
	her voice fades away.

In this example, it can be seen that the change in speech reflects a change in awareness, expresses the *recognition* of some difficulty or hindrance, and then *anticipates* its solution. Speech here appears to change from providing a *monitoring* of action to *directing* the child's own action, and perhaps anticipates *planning* ahead, before there is a return to what seems to be a use of language for monitoring the child's play once more.

Luria's research shows how language helps the child to direct his attention and focus on his action, bringing it under his control, in situations in which he finds difficulty in pacing, or being precise with his action. Luria refers to this characteristic of language as the *pragmatic, directive function* and in a series of experiments has shown how this function relates to the 'significative or generalising function of the word' (Luria, 1961, p. 351). Three-year-old children were asked to respond to a panel of lights by pressing a ball when the red light came on, and by not pressing the ball when a blue light came on. Although at this age the child is unable to accomplish this task on his own, when reinforced by 'press' or 'don't press' from the adult, the task comes within his control.

When asked to instruct himself it seems that the 3-year-old child is unable to give the instruction and perform the action, that is, verbalising inhibits action, but by the age of 4 only the words 'don't press' inhibit the action.

There are many examples in the data of children using language to focus attention on the actions they are trying to perform. Jane in the following example is trying to turn on the taps of the toy bath. They are very small and stiff.

Jane:	Having a bath, and I'm . . .	Jane struggles with the tap.
	turning . . . it, turning . . .	She paces her efforts and
	it. It won't turn.	concentrates attention with
Ann:	Let me try.	each word she utters.
Jane:	No . . . I can . . . turn . . . it . . .	The pressure is in the words
	and turn . . . it . . . a bit . . .	and in the action.
	a bit . . . and there it's on.	

This example illustrates the strategy of *focusing attention* and concentrating on precise, sustained or intricate action.

A third strategy that appears may be referred to as *forward planning*. This strategy serves to review a plan of action before it is embarked upon, and may anticipate difficulties and plan to meet them. For example:

Jim: I am going to cut the clay to make two
       bits . . . the same . . . Then I'll flatten
       them out . . . well one goes at each end.

There is considerable support from the data that much of the young child's
talk is concerned with his own actions, and serves to monitor, direct,
anticipate and plan his own actions.

THE OTHER DIRECTING USE OF LANGUAGE

The directive function is also evident when language is used for directing
the actions of others or for directing the self in conjunction with others.
   A strategy that is seen frequently is one of *demonstration* and *running
commentary*, for example:

Tim: Put your car in there like that.
       That's right . . . now *you* put a brick
       at the door like this.

   Or the strategy may be one of *instructing*, for example:

James: Put your brick right on top.
         Be careful . . . don't push it . . .
         go and get a flag now . . .
         fasten it on top with a slide.

   A third strategy when directing others is one of *forward planning* of the
other persons actions, for example:

James: You'll have to get another piece . . .
         a white one and little . . . and
         then you'll have to put a pin in
         the box over there . . . to fasten it on
         with.

   A further strategy is evident when directing others leads to *collaborating*,
that is, when a series of actions in which others, or the self and others, are
taking part, is anticipated and there is forward planning for joint or shared
action, as in the following example:
   Tom and Peter are playing side by side. Peter is engrossed in trying to
push a tyre back on to a wheel of his car.

1 *Tom*:	Turning the wheel like this . . . round . . . brr . . . on a road . . . on a road . . . put a brick on top.	Tom is pushing a lorry round the floor. He seems unaware of

2	Careful ... just put ... it ... gently ... a brick on ... fetch some bricks.	Peter and the observer, but concentrates on placing brick on top of wall.
3	Down there look ... I'm going to pile a lot of bricks to have a crash.	Tom straightens up – speaks more loudly then reaches for the bricks. He begins to pile up the bricks.
4	Pete I'm going to put a big pile here ... put them on top ... like this ... you bring yours ... you build the wall ... make it high with those bricks ... make a track round it.	Peter abandons his efforts with the tyre and watches Tom.
Peter:	I'm bringing some bricks for it ... there, putting them on top of those.	Peter brings some bricks and begins to build.
5 *Tom:*	Then we'll have to be careful ... we'll ...	Tom waits for Peter to put his bricks on the wall and then continues building.
6 *Peter:*	Build it there ... you can put them on top there, there done it ... now ... sending the car round the corner fast.	Peter picks up the car and pushes it.
7 *Tom:*	Mine will ... and it can't see yours coming ... so you will have to watch.	Tom is still piling up bricks.
8 *Peter*	There's going to be a crash ... build yours up high now then we can make them crash together.	

This last example illustrates the use of language and some of the strategies that children employ which are evidence of the directive function of language. At (1) we see the self-directing use in which at first the strategy of monitoring is used, then at (2) gives way to a focusing strategy that appears to be controlling the child's physical manipulative action as he places the brick without causing the wall to fall. Then at (3) the strategy of forward planning of the self's actions appears, before giving way at (4) to the other-directing use of language as Tom first uses a strategy of demonstration – 'put them on top like this' – and then a strategy of instruction 'you bring yours ... you build the wall ... make it high'. We then see at (5) that Tom tries to establish joint action, a strategy that is attempting collaboration and finally at (6), (7) and (8) we perhaps see, on the part of both Tom and Peter, strategies that might be regarded as approaching collaborative forward planning.

This last example illustrates clearly the way in which two functions are served by the child's language. Action is directed and carried out, but also the relationships between the two boys is communicated, one that might be judged to be one of *equality* and *mutual concern*. We shall discuss this aspect more fully in the next chapter.

THE INTERPRETATIVE FUNCTION

If a large part of the child's language is concerned with his own action and activities, there is another large section that is the reflection of the meaning that the scene, and events around him, have for him. We refer to this as the interpretative function and it emerges in two uses of language that appear to reflect the awareness of different levels of complexity in the structure the child is able to place on his experiences. The two uses of language serving the interpretative function are the reporting use and the reasoning use.

REPORTING

Much of the 3-year-old's talk seems to serve to identify objects and events that the child views; almost as though it mirrors for him the visual scene. For example:

Mark: That's a cowboy and that's an Indian.
          There's a see-saw . . . and
          it goes up and down, doesn't it?
          It's snowing now . . .
          it's snowing . . .
          on the tree . . .
          it's a Christmas tree.

This is using language to represent items and events that the child observes, indicating those aspects of the scene around him that engage his attention. His language reflects those features of his immediate experience that have significance for him as he reports on his ongoing experiences. The same use appears to serve the child in his recall of past experiences. As the child remembers some experience, it would appear that he has an image of the earlier event which he can, as it were, inspect, selecting significant features to represent through language. He provides labels or identification of particular components of the recalled experience as though he were making a report of the scene. The following are examples of reporting past experience:

Alan:　My grannie's got one . . . a cat . . . got a cat
　　　　and it scratched me . . . on my leg it scratched.
Tim:　I saw a big ship . . . and it was going on the sea.
　　　　It had some chimneys . . . and smoke out.

Reporting can be at a minimal level, where the strategy used is one of labelling the components of the scene, for example 'A cat and a dog, a girl and a boy and that's a daddy'. But interpretations can reach a different level when the child adopts an analytical approach that distinguishes components of the situation on the basis of detail and relationships. As the child examines the scene before him he may adopt more than one strategy in his attempt to make an interpretation. Examples of the strategies that were used by 3-year-olds are given below.

Analytical strategies

　　1 *The elaboration of detail*
James talks about his visit to the seaside.

James:　We went in the sea . . .
　　　　　and it was cold . . . and it splashed.
　　　　　There was a lot of little things . . .
　　　　　I saw them . . . little fishes swimming.

　　2 *By association with some earlier experience and making comparisons*
John compares the snowstorm with his own which is not present.

John:　I've got one of those . . . but it's not like
　　　　that one . . . my one's not got an Indian in it like that.
　　　　Tim compares the tractor he is looking at with
　　　　one he has met earlier.

Tim:　This tractor's got big wheels but I've
　　　　seen one that's got bigger and bigger
　　　　wheels – and giant big tyres.

　　3 *The recognition of incongruity*

Tom:　The garage is too small for the car to go in.

　　4 *The awareness of sequence*

Jane:　And we went on a holiday . . . and I was poorly with
　　　　measles. Then Bobby got the measles . . . but we're
　　　　all better now.

3

5 *The recognition of associated action or events*

Jane:　And the man was walking across the road . . . and a
car came and the policeman put his hand up
and stopped it to let him go

6 *By the absence of conditions*

Tom:　It didn't have big wheels and it couldn't go
very fast

These uses provide evidence of the child's growing inclination to make
some analysis and so place a fuller interpretation on his experiences. The
attention to detail (present or absent), the making of comparisons, the
interpretation of actions, the reference to sequence, making associations
and the recognition of incongruity are all part of the analytical behaviour
that is necessary if extended meaning for experiences is to be extracted, that
is, if experience is to be organised as a complex structure.

In addition to analytical strategies there are also synthesising strategies,
for example:

7 *The recognition of a central meaning*
James, as he looks into the snowstorm:

There's a fight going on in the snow. The Indian's
shooting at the cowboy and trying to kill him.

John, as Mark accidently knocks over his blocks:

You've knocked the chimney off and you're spoiling
my building. It needs mending now.

8 *Reflecting on the meaning of experience*

I didn't like it in the water . . . it was cold and horrible . . .
and I wanted to get out and get dried.

REASONING

The use of language for reasoning seems to develop from reporting in
which attention is given to several aspects of the situation reported on. The
reasoning use employs logical thought and argument, and the strategies
used include the *recognition of underlying principles*, and of *cause and effect
relationships*. Such relationships are recognised perhaps as a result of the
analytical approach. Three-year-olds are not yet using language for logical

reasoning but there are some examples in the data that show that some children are capable of using language in an attempt to make a reasoned interpretation of their experiences and this is important, even though their reasoning may be illogical.

Two strategies can be illustrated by examples from the 3-year-olds' talk.

1 *The recognition of causal relationships*

Mark: I broke it . . . I was running and I fell . . . on my dad's
fireplace . . . and that's how it broke.

Tom: And if you break your arm or your leg . . . you've to
go to hospital to get it mended.

Jane: And the ice cream was all soft 'cos we forgot to
put it in the fridge.

2 *The recognition of a principle or a condition*

John: My grannie died . . . she was poorly and she was
very old . . . so she died.

Andrew: People don't like you if you take their things . . .
I don't do that.

The interpretative function of language is revealed, then, through the reporting and reasoning uses of language, and the strategies reflect the different means by which the child recognises and organises his experiences into a meaningful structure. The strategies he uses suggest different directions in the focus of attention: he centres upon detail, or he may relate one part to another, or set it against the whole. At the simplest level the strategy of labelling or identifying seems only to parallel what the child sees or touches: at the most complex level, the strategy of synthesising and recognising principles and causal relationships is dependent on analytical activity that may or may not be fully expressed in language. The interpretative function of language is the one that deals with the world outside oneself and reflects the ability to scan, analyse and recognise relationships and to impose order on the scenes and events which make up experience.

THE PROJECTIVE FUNCTION

The third of the ideational functions that language appears to serve is the projective function. It is concerned with the organisation of meaning for events that have not yet occurred and which may never take place. All meaning must be based on earlier experience of some kind, but the projective function of language draws on relevant earlier experience and, through the use of the imagination, supports attempts to explore events that are still in the future, or savour what it feels like to be another person, or take part in a situation which occurs only in the imagination. We refer to this kind of mental activity as projective, since it is an endeavour to extend thinking beyond immediate or personal experience.

Three uses of language appear to be a realisation of the projective function, the *predictive* use that anticipates possible happenings in the future or contemplates events that are remote, the *empathetic* use that is an attempt to savour the life and feelings of other people and the *imaginative* use that is concerned with experiencing events that exist only in the imagination.

In considering the strategies that appear in the projective uses of language, it is clear that they are much the same as those that serve the interpretative function, and may be at a level either of reporting or of reasoning, but when serving the projective function, the characteristic is that the thinking extends beyond the immediate present or past experiences, and there is an element of conjecture, and a dependency on the imagination for its existence.

PREDICTING

There are a few examples of this use of language in the talk of 3-year-olds, but it seems that many 3-year-olds are not yet able to use language for this purpose. It involves projecting beyond the present experience and employs strategies that of necessity anticipate events in the future or project into events that are not part of direct experience. A number of strategies appear in the talk of 3-year-olds, as illustrated in the following examples.

1 *Forecasting* appears frequently in the talk of some children. Jill is talking about her playmate Alison who doesn't yet go to school.

Jill: Wait until she's four or eight and then she'll go
      to school and she'll be a new person to go to school.
Mary: My dad's going to make me a see-saw . . . when it's
      summer he's going to.
Alan: There's roundabouts coming too. We soon . . . and
      I'm going on them.

2 *Anticipating consequences* is a strategy which appeared infrequently in the language of 3-year-olds.

Meg: My mam'll be cross 'cos I've got my sleeves wet.
Timmie: You'll fall and hurt your head if you don't hold
      tight.

3 Sometimes the 3-year-old child shows that he can *survey possible alternatives*, for example:

Jill: We might get a cat one day . . . but I think we'll
           get a hamster first.
James: Well we could go on a bus or a train to my auntie's.
           I don't know which.

4 And sometimes the child predicts *related possibilities* about something that might happen.

Mary: If the man runs fast he might jump on that bus.
Peter: (looking at the snowstorm) If it's got a crack in
           it the water might come out.

5 Finally a strategy that would seem to be part of the predictive use is the *recognition of problems and the prediction of solutions*. There were few instances of this in the talk of the 3-year-olds, but perhaps the following examples show that it is coming within reach.

Adrian: It won't fasten on now it's broked . . . it won't
           pull it either.
           I think some string would do . . . some string
           can mend it.

THE EMPATHETIC USE OF LANGUAGE

The second use of language that arises from the projective function is the empathetic use. It is concerned with imagining and expressing the feelings and the reactions of other people to their experiences. Role playing might be considered an attempt to discover what it is like to be another person, but in his imaginative role play the child is usually imitating the characteristic features of the role and is not likely to be contemplating how the people he imitates might feel: he is much more concerned with the pleasure he himself is getting from the imitated behaviour and we would include this within the imaginative use of language.

At times, however, we can see that even 3-year-olds do become concerned about how others feel and perhaps draw on memories of what their own reactions would be in similar circumstances; or perhaps it is that they are reacting on behalf of the other person, that is, imagining the situation is happening to them, identifying themselves with the other person. Whatever the basis is, the child is clearly projecting, and is imposing meanings and expressing them through language, and this provides evidence of the empathetic use of language. The following are examples taken from the talk of 3-year-olds.

1 Jane refers to a child who was crying before she came into the observation room:

Jane: She doesn't like Terry teasing . . . that's horrible . . . and she's crying 'cos she didn't like it.

2 Tim talks about the figures in the snowstorm novelty:

Tim: The cowboy wouldn't like going up and down on the see-saw . . . it would make him feel sick.

Michelle is telling the observer about an accident at home when her mother fell over their dog:

Michelle: Lassie didn't mean to . . . not to hurt my mum . . . she didn't.

This last example is perhaps an attempt to consider the problems for both the mother and the dog.

In the talk of the 3-year-olds in the project, the empathetic use did not appear frequently. It may be that this was due to the character of the play situation or it may be due more to the characteristics of 3-year-olds. This latter explanation seems to be the most likely, since we have considerable evidence from the work of Piaget of the young child's inability to take into account the viewpoint of his listeners as he talks to them (Piaget, 1923). The young child is still struggling to establish his own view of experiences and it is perhaps to be expected that he cannot easily recognise that others may see things quite differently. We would not therefore expect the empathetic use to occur frequently in the talk of 3-year-olds.

IMAGINING

If the predictive and empathetic uses are not frequently evident in the talk of 3-year-olds, the imaginative use is frequently seen as the child plays alone or with other children. Most children seem to engage in representational play very readily. They pick up materials or objects and rename them, pieces of wood become boats, boxes become buildings, sticks become guns. The child renames the material and by his actions indicates that he is regarding the material as a symbol for the actuality. Amongst the 3-year-olds recorded there was not one who did not use language to rename materials and indicate that he was setting up a scene in his imagination.

There are many examples of language used as a *representing* or *renaming* strategy, for example:

John puts two small boxes on the floor:

John: That's for a house where the man lives ... and
that's ones for the car ... a garage.

Alan takes up a large block.

Alan: It's an aeroplane ... going over ... brr-rr ...
it's coming to land brr-rr.

Sue picks up a toilet roll.

Sue: This is a policeman coming ... coming to see the fire.

There is also a great deal of language used by some 3-year-olds that refers to objects, scenes and incidents and there is nothing to serve as representations or symbols. Words alone are the observable evidence of the scene, or incident, that the child is building up through his imagination, and to which he responds as though it were an ongoing actuality. These children are using language to give a *commentary* on the imagined context of their play.

Often some materials will provide a representational basis in the initial stage, but ideas are then extended and words alone become the means of making the extension to the scene. The following are examples:

1 *Jill*: My baby's poorly ... doctor ... will you come quickly ...
will you give her something special ... give her a
prick thing to make her better.
2 *Dan*: Here's the van coming ... it's taking all the washing
round. Here you are Mrs ... here's your washing ...
money please ... thank you.
3 *Tom*: The building's all on fire ... a man at the top ...
can't get down ... fire engine comes ... er-er-er-er- ...
get out the ladder ... put it up ... the fire's
burning ... get the man down ... down.
4 *John*: There's a boat coming ... brrrr ... it's started ... it's
coming on the water ... a big wave ... a big wave ... the
people nearly fall into the water.

In each of these examples there is little material present to be used symbolically. In the first example another child is taking the role of the baby, but there is no telephone – the position of Jill's hand indicates that she is imagining using a telephone. In the second example, Dan is pushing a small van around the legs of a stool. There is nothing to represent either washing or money or ladies. In the third example, two small upturned boxes seem to represent the building and a small brick on top of a larger one is pushed round to represent a fire engine. There is no ladder, no man, no fire and nothing to represent them save the words the child uses.

In the last example, John is standing in a wooden box, swaying and using his hands a great deal, but there is nothing to represent water or waves or people, except his gestures and his words.

These examples illustrate again the way in which strategies of language serve different uses and different functions. In many examples of the imaginative use of language we can distinguish evidence of other functions, both the directive and the interpretative functions, and the characteristic strategies of the uses within these functions are prominent. The interpretative function may be realised within the imagined context and the uses and strategies of reporting and logical reasoning may also be present. Similarly the directive function may be realised within the imagined context and the child may be directing actions and planning ahead within his imagined role.

The ideational functions of language, the directive, the interpretative and the projective, provided a framework within which the meaning expressed in the major part of the talk of 3-year-olds can be accounted for.

We shall turn to a discussion of the fourth section of the classification – the relational function – in the next chapter.

Chapter 6

The Relational Function

The relationships that are assumed when people talk with one another and the way in which those relationships are expressed have provided a major interest for the social sciences during the last decade.

As we have already seen, a major contribution to our understanding has, without doubt, come from the work of Basil Bernstein and his associates. Their contribution has taken the form of empirical and theoretical studies, which at times have provoked heated debate.

We have already referred to the conflict that has arisen, which seems to result from detaching the model that Bernstein has developed as a basis for classifying language data from the theoretical argument upon which it is founded. Yet it is Bernstein's theoretical framework and the insights that are derived from it that have brought new understanding of the way in which different social groups come to use language so differently. Although the model may be inadequate, nevertheless, when taken with the underlying theory and projected into the actuality of linguistic interaction, it gains support from what is observed.

We have already indicated that Bernstein has been very much influenced by the Sapir–Whorf approach in which language is seen to have a tremendous influence on the developing members of any social group: it is 'a great force of socialisation, probably the greatest that exists' (Sapir, 1921). The way in which the individual comes to perceive and respond to the world around him is largely a result of his experiences of the language forms and patterns used by the group to which he belongs: thus he is likely to come to use language in the same way, and the meanings that underlie those forms and patterns will be induced as a result of the experiences shared by the group. His linguistic experiences will shape his inner frames of reference, which are the means by which he interprets all new experiences. This is essentially the view put forward by Whorf (1956). The particular forms and patterns of language to which the child is exposed carry values and attitudes, and serve to focus the child's attention on to aspects of his experience that those who talk with him see as significant, or that are unchallenged tenets of a way of life.

In developing a programme of research that has sought to test this theory, Bernstein has produced empirical evidence to show that adolescent boys from different social groups have different orientations towards their experiences and set different interpretations on them. Although Bernstein sees such differences as evidence of the existence of different meaning systems (referred to more recently as the 'deep structure' of the language), nevertheless the differences are to be inferred from the expression of those meanings in speech forms. Thus the 'code', or underlying meaning, is to be recognised from the use of particular linguistic features. Since a list of features which provide clues to the speaker's inner 'code' has been formally set out, these features inevitably have come to be seen as the codes themselves (Bernstein, 1961). It is this assumption that meanings have a direct relationship to formal linguistic features that has led others, particularly Labov (1970) and Rosen (1972), to accuse Bernstein of making an issue out of aspects of language use that are nothing more than differences in linguistic styles.

But if the notion of codes is accepted as being, as Bernstein has recently reiterated, related to underlying meanings or 'deep structures', then we can proceed to a consideration of the basic concept in his theory, that of the differences between social groups in the relationships that are assumed, and induced, between members of the family, which may account for some differences in the way in which language is used by children.

Bernstein predicts what will be the effects on children of two basically opposed positions from which the mother may see the child, positions that stem from the attitudes and perspectives that are associated with socio-economic status. Where the mother regards relationships as fixed and unalterable, governed by the authority which her position in the family confers on her, then she is likely to see the child as occupying an inferior position to herself and be mainly concerned to establish her authority as mother. The relationship she is likely to take up is one described by Bernstein as 'positional': in her dealings with the child she is likely to pass on that information that the child needs in order to recognise and conform to his mother's authority. Thus she will operate as though there is an 'ideal' child who recognises her authority and realises his own role. When the child fails to comply with this model, she will seek to inform him of the appropriate behaviour of a child. Thus she may appeal to him to be 'a good boy', 'a big boy', or to have those qualities to be admired in a child, to be 'not dirty', 'not rude', 'not disobedient', to do as mother tells him, to accept authority. In this way the child is helped to learn his place, or role, within the family. Not only this, in making his role clear to him the mother will inform him about the roles of others, for example that fathers will punish children, that older children have certain privileges that younger children have not. Within a position-oriented family the behaviour appropriate to the position of each child in the family will be made clear by example, and, as parents seek to control the child's behaviour, they will appeal to him to behave acceptably, by referring to the characteristics of his role, and to the status and power of other members of the family. In learning his own role the child learns also the fixed relationships between himself and other members, and if he does not comply willingly then attempts at enforcement are likely to follow.

But there are other ways of viewing the child. He may be seen as an individual but immature person, who one day will take on the skills, character and responsibilities of an adult. This view would see the child as a potential adult needing to learn how to be an adult and gradually moving towards this. Thus the view of the mother towards him might be regarded as 'person'-oriented. Clearly this mother also has in mind the 'ideal' child who by agreement chooses to behave as an adult. He is expected almost to take an adult view of himself as a child. Thus it is explained to him why he cannot do the things adults do because he is still a child and he is expected to agree to his own control and regulation. It is the appeal for agreement that characterises the 'person'-oriented relationship between mother and child. When the child fails to comply with the mother's expectation, the appeal is to his reason: 'You must go to bed now because you will be very tired in the morning if you don't have enough sleep.' 'Don't take baby's toys because he's only little and he doesn't understand that you're only borrowing them for a while.'

When he fails to meet the parents' expectations the child is likely to have explained to him the acceptable basis for making relationships and to regard the other as a person who must also have choices open to him. The basis of relationships in a family of this kind is the projection into the other's feelings and anticipated responses, and the recognition of the other's part in the relationship.

Thus the child in the person-oriented family is learning to be person-oriented also. It would seem that it is the need to have the child understand the basis of acceptable behaviour that leads to explicitness on the part of the parents, and exposes the child to the exploration of the meanings of relationships between members of the family through the use of language.

But the differences in the relationship between mothers and their children may be of a wider significance than the way in which the child is controlled. The position-oriented mother is likely to see the child as a child and to infer that there is little knowledge within his reach. She expects him to play with other children because this is a traditional activity for young children, so she releases him from her control quite readily. The parents may not see the child as a developing person to whom knowledge should be made accessible and so may be doing little to help him acquire basic everyday knowledge.

The person-oriented mother will see her child as a developing individual who is learning to share in the interests of other members of the family. Thus she tries to make knowledge available to him. She explains phenomena as they arise, they look at books, she is alert to what will interest him, and it all becomes part of her control strategies: appeal to reason, appeal to interest, appeal to participation and agreement and to the basic principles that govern their relationship.

These then seem to be the contrasting relationships that mothers can take up with their children. But in practice these two positions are likely to be poles of behaviour between which mothers might operate. It may be true that some mothers operate only within the positional orientation. Other mothers may take up a person-oriented position until the point of breakdown in the relationship, when the child fails to agree to his own control, and only then will the parent assume positional control. This seems likely to be the position that many parents take, saying the equivalent of 'I asked you to be sensible and go to bed now. If you don't accept reasons then you must accept that I am your mother, and know what's best, so just go to bed now – or I shall have to enforce it. Go to bed because I say so – now.'

The persistence of the appeal to the child for agreement will vary – for some the switch from person appeal to position assertion may be very sharp. For others the person appeal period may be prolonged, and the child may be given reasons and explanations until the adult's patience is exhausted; then may come a regretful summary of the child's failure to be like an adult, or 'sensible', or 'helpful', before the authority of the adult is imposed.

Parents have different priorities and different kinds of explanations may be given. The basis of the appeal for agreement may range from concern for the child's own well-being, or the well-being of parents, brothers, sisters or other people, to the encouragement of greater competence, or for the need to achieve or surpass some standard set by others. It seems likely that the child will be exposed to ideas and will have the responsibility for his choice of action set before him at some time.

It is from such experiences in the home that the child will establish ways of talking that reflect the kinds of relationships that members of his family demonstrate are appropriate as they talk to each other. The view of the child that the mother takes will tend to determine not only how he will be addressed, but the kinds of information that will be made clear to him. It is the relationships that have been established between adult and child in the home that will determine how the child will learn to view the other and that will be made evident by the strategies he selects for expressing meanings. The strategies that the child selects to express relationships as he talks with another are likely to influence the kind of interaction which will emerge. We refer then to this function of language as the *relational* function, and it would seem that it is realised through two uses of language which we refer to as the *self-maintaining* and the *interactional* uses of language.

In an earlier paper (Tough, 1973b), in which the framework for the classification of the uses of language was first discussed, we proposed that two related functions, the relational and the self-maintaining, should be recognised as serving to convey, establish and maintain relationships between people. On further consideration of the framework, however, it seems that the one function, the relational function, best fits our definition of 'function', and the different means by which language serves to indicate the way in which the child is relating himself to others would more appropriately be explained through the uses of language, that is through the self-maintaining and the interactional uses of language.

THE SELF-MAINTAINING USE OF LANGUAGE

How does the child view himself in relation to others? All children are seeking for recognition as people who matter; all have needs, both physical and psychological needs, and all children seek to establish their rights and worth in the eyes of other people. Much of the child's use of language is concerned, then, with making others aware of him as a person, and in gaining attention and recognition. His needs are made explicit through language. This use of language might be seen as maintaining the self in relation to other people and might therefore be considered as one realisation of the relational function of language.

The kind of strategies that the child will use in his attempts at self-maintenance will be:

1 *Expression of need*
This will refer to both physical and psychological needs, that is, with personal comfort and success, and with maintaining the status of the self in the eyes of others, for example: 'I want a biscuit' 'Can I have a sweet?' It will include strategies which aim to draw attention to the self: 'Watch me, see what I'm doing' or 'Aren't I clever'.

2 *Protection of self-interest*
This aims to protect the self and the rights and property of the self, for example: 'Go away – you're hurting me', 'That's my car – you can't have it', 'Please don't spoil my picture'.

3 *Justifications*
These are strategies which do not appear frequently in the language of 3-year-olds. They express the child's attempts to place his demands or protests in a rational argument, for example: 'I want a red crayon so I can draw my picture better', 'Don't take all the bricks 'cos I need some more to finish my castle'.

Other strategies will aim to maintain the child's status with others by, as it were, attacking others, and trying to convey a sense of his own superiority. Thus we will find:

4 *Criticisms*

For example: 'I don't like your picture', 'You're naughty', 'Cry baby', 'Your castle isn't as big as mine'. There might, also, be implied criticism, for example: 'It might be better if you painted it blue'.

5 *Threats*

For example: 'Give me a sweet or I'll hit you', 'If you spoil my castle I'll have to tell the teacher'.

THE INTERACTIONAL USE OF LANGUAGE

It seems at first, perhaps, that the self-maintaining use of language would account adequately for the expression of the relationships that the child is setting up with others as he talks. But how might we distinguish the following examples taken from the recorded talk of 3-year-olds?

1 Give me it that car it's mine.
2 Would you give me my car back now please 'cos I'm going home.

We can see that both utterances have the same goal, that is to retrieve the car. They are both seeking to protect the interests of the self and in this sense are indicating the relationships in which they see themselves with others. There are differences, however, in the way in which these two utterances approach the other person.

Some perhaps would argue that the two utterances above have the same meaning and that any difference is in style and not in meaning. But this seems to confuse the goal with the meaning. Without doubt the children have the same goal in mind, to retrieve a car. But the meaning of the situation is not necessarily the same for the children. For the one the focus of attention is on his rights and the trespass the other has done. He does not project into the listener's position or into his feelings, but makes a direct demand, irrespective of the reaction of the other child.

But the second child focuses attention on the other; he seeks agreement. The meaning the situation has for him is one that includes the anticipated effect on the other, the recognition perhaps that there is more likely to be agreement if he lays out the justification for his claim. Even though it may be argued that each child is acting without deliberation and is using phrases in familiar strategies, this does not prove that meaning for the two children is the same: to do so would be to suggest that the focus of the relationship contributes nothing to meaning. We would argue that the presentation of justifications and the appeal to the other are indications of the meaning of that situation for the child and are clearly different in meaning from those occasions when the same child would be so upset at the sight of someone with one of his possessions that he would fly at the other with the demand 'Give me it, it's mine'. The fact that he selects one strategy rather than another in situations that are clearly different seems to indicate that there is a difference in the meaning of the two forms for him. It is, of course, true that strategy may be used because the child recognises that it is expected of him in certain situations, for example, that sanctions may be applied if he uses an aggressive, coercive strategy; but even so the selected strategy must reflect something of the meaning of the situation for the child.

It seems, therefore, that the way in which the approach to the other is made and the way in which the other's approach is received contribute something more to communication in terms of assumed relationships. The expression of these assumed relationships may determine the kind of interaction that takes place. We refer then to this use of language as the interactional use.

The strategies that may be used will range from those that centre entirely on the speaker's view of the situation, as in 'Give me the car it's mine', to those that clearly take into account the other person's point of view, as in the second example 'Would you like to give me my car back now,' 'cos I'm going home'.

In the analysis of the 3-year-olds' use of language, which we report in the next chapter, we have included the self-maintaining use of language as part of the classification, but at the time we could not find a satisfactory way of including the interactional use of language in the analysis. In a subsequent book, however, we shall deal in some detail with this aspect of the use of language (Tough and Sestini, in preparation).

The relational function, together with the directive function, the interpretative function and the projective function, formed the basis of the classification that was used for the analysis of the recorded talk of the 3-year-olds in the study. It does not seem likely that the classification is exhaustive, or would be entirely appropriate for the analysis of adult's language, but it provided a set of descriptions of language in use that could be used objectively and which offered a basis for comparing the language used by different children. A summary of the framework is given in the following pages.

A framework for the classification of the uses of language

Function	Uses of language	Strategies
The directive function	1. Self-directing	i monitoring actions ii focusing control iii forward planning
	2. Other-directing	i demonstrating ii instructing iii forward planning iv anticipating collaborative action (self and other)
The interpretative function	1. Reporting on present and past experiences	i labelling *analytical strategies including*: ii elaboration of detail iii association and comparison iv recognising incongruity v awareness of sequence vi recognition of associated actions or events vii absence of conditions viii recognition of a central meaning ix reflecting on the meaning of experiences
	2. Reasoning	i recognising dependent and causal relationships ii the recognition of a principle or determining conditions
The projective function	1. Predicting	i forecasting events ii anticipating consequences iii surveying possible alternatives iv forecasting related possibities v recognition of problems and predicting solutions

Function	Uses of language	Strategies
	2. Empathetic	i projecting into experiences of others ii projecting into other people's feelings iii anticipating reactions of others
	3. Imaginating	i renaming ii commentary on imagined context iii building scene through language iv language of role (strategies of the directive and interpretative functions will be used within imagined contexts)
The relational function	1. Self-maintaining	i referring to needs ii protection of self-interest iii justification iv criticism v threats
	2. Interactional	i self-emphasising strategies ii other-recognising strategies

Chapter 7

The Analysis of 3-Year-Olds' Use of Language

The classification outlined in the last chapter formed the framework for the analysis of the recorded talk of the 3-year-olds in the study. Almost all the utterances could be assigned with confidence to three functions, the directive function, the interpretative function and the projective function, or to the self-maintaining use of language, which we have regarded as a realisation of the relational function.

We considered the other realisation of the relational function, the interactional use of language, separately, since we could not at that time find a satisfactory method of analysis, which would take account of this aspect of the functioning of language at the same time as accounting for the purposes for which children were using language.

In order to illustrate the way in which utterances were classified we shall discuss excerpts from two transcriptions. These excerpts will not only demonstrate the kind of data we were dealing with, but also indicate the differences in orientation towards the use of language that seemed to be developing between the advantaged and the disadvantaged groups of children.

EXCERPT 1

Billy and Michele have set out the dolls' furniture and the family of dolls is being introduced to the setting.

1	Billy:	Look what I've got.
2	Michele:	I've got one as well.
3	Billy:	It's a mister.
4	Michele:	Mine isn't it's a lady ...
5		... Putting her there ...
6		I'm making it go there.
7	Billy:	Give her here ... I want it.
8	Michele:	No ... it's mine.
9	Billy:	Well I've got this one
10		... he's getting on this ...
11		... it's falling off look.
		(He puts the doll on top of a lorry)
12		Watch me do this Michele.

13 *Michele*:   You'll have to watch out baby Thompson.
              (Billy pushes the car in through the furniture)
14   Hey give up . . . that's mine.
15 *Billy*:   Pushing it into the house . . .
16   It's knocking it all over.
17 *Michele*:   This girl wants a ride . . .
              (She puts the girl on the lorry)
18 *Billy*:   They're both having a ride.
              (He pushes the car round and round)
19   Put that car there Michele.
20   Push it to this.
21 *Michele*:   It's coming, it's coming, it'll hit yours.
22 *Billy*:   Make it come . . . hit it . . . there.

The talk here between Billy and Michele is characteristic of much of the talk of the 3-year-olds that was recorded as they played. We shall consider now how it might be placed within the classification. There were no problems in this example of deciding what should be recognised as an utterance. In parts the children are following the turn and turn about order of conversation, so that they expect to begin and finish what they have to say and then wait for the other. This is not always the case, however, and at times there would be an overlap of voices as one child interrupted another, or when children became absorbed in their own meanings and talked mainly for themselves and they were then no longer expecting answers and were not aware of the comments which others were making.

In this example there are pauses (indicated by . . .) that are long enough for the listener to assume that the sequences have been generated at successive points, and do not originate from one underlying 'sentence'.

Several of the utterances are concerned with the child's efforts to gain recognition for himself and so are classified as self-maintaining.

For example, Billy attempts to gain Michele's attention:

1 *Billy*:   Look what I've got.
12 *Billy*:   Watch me do this Michele.

which bring responses from Michele that indicate that she is vying with Billy for recognition, for example:

2 *Michele*:   I've got one as well.

Other utterances that would be classified as self-maintaining are concerned with establishing ownership or taking possession, or preventing trespass on one's rights or property, for example:

7	*Billy*:	Give it here . . . I want it.
8	*Michele*:	No it's mine.
9	*Billy*:	Well I've got this one.
14	*Michele*:	Hey give up . . . that's mine.

Other evidence of the self-maintaining function would be found in the use of criticism, abuse or threats to the other and in assertions of superiority. In the example below there is just one example of abuse or threat, a strategy of coercion.

13	*Michele*:	You'll have to watch out baby Thompson.

Perhaps the presence of the observer prevented further conflict between the children.

The remainder of the utterances in the example fall into other categories. First there are statements about the child's actions that seem to parallel what the child is doing, almost as though he is monitoring his own actions.

5	*Michele*:	Putting her there.
6		I'm making it go there.
15	*Billy*:	Pushing it into the house . . .
16		It's knocking it all over.

This use of language would seem to be that referred to by Lewis as synpractic and is evidence of the directive function, the self-directing use of language, and the strategy is monitoring action.

Several of the children's comments are evidence of the interpretative function. The child gives a commentary or report on the scene in front of him.

3	*Billy*:	It's a mister.
4	*Michele*:	Mine isn't . . . it's a lady.
9	*Billy*:	Well I've got this one
11		it's falling off look.

We can see here that the children are interpreting the present experience and are reporting on it. Although we would place this within the reporting use, the interpretation is clearly at the minimal level of labelling. The strategy is one of identifying components of the scene and placing labels on them, for example 'lady', 'mister', and 'falling off'.

There is also evidence of the projective function, realised through the imaginative use of language, for the children show through their talk that they are operating within an imagined context. The imagined scene is not developed through the use of language, however, but they clearly assign an imagined role to the figures they are manipulating.

10 *Billy*:   He's getting on this.
17 *Michele*:   This girl wants a ride.

In both cases the children use a minimum level of interpretation and only identify objects and actions in the imagined scene. These utterances would, therefore, be classified as lying within the projective function, within the imaginative use of language, and using a strategy of monitoring and labelling.

Thus we can see that each utterance in this excerpt has been assigned to a particular function, to a particular use of language, and to a particular strategy. There may be some problems in making decisions when more than one strategy is used within an utterance, or sometimes when the characteristic features of more than one use of language occur, as in the following example:

John: That's a bike, and that's its saddle, and those are the pedals that you have to push round and round with your feet to make it go when you ride it.

In the first part of this utterance we can see that a strategy of labelling is used, but in the second part John associates actions and events in order to express his understanding of how a bicycle works. This utterance would be allocated to the more complex of the two strategies, that of associating actions and events, to the reporting use of language and to the interpretative function.

In the first extract the children are using language for several purposes, and at the same time it is serving the relational function, as the relationships that each child intuitively is assuming as he speaks with the other find expression through the interactional use of language. For the most part the relationship is one of equality, for although both use the imperative form it would not seem to be for the purpose of indicating status differences between them. There are occasions when the strategy is one of self-assertion, and none of the utterances employ other-recognising strategies. Each utterance can be examined and the strategies that children are using to serve the interactional use can be classified. This analysis, however, was not completed for the 3-year-olds' talk but will be a topic for discussion in the later publication.

This extract was typical of much of the conversation of 3-year-olds and the major part of the talk of children in the disadvantaged group was of this kind. The amount of talk at this level, however, varied a good deal from child to child in the advantaged group but all used language for purposes that are illustrated in the following transcription.

EXCERPT 2

EXTRACT FROM RECORDED PLAY SESSION

Tom, who is nearly 3½, and Sally, who is 3 years and 4 months, are playing together on a low table with the project's play materials. The observer is sitting alongside, making notes on aspects of the children's play. Tom has picked up the snowstorm novelty and Sally is looking at it with him.

1 *Tom*:   Look there's a man . . . (Sally tries to take the novelty from him)
            Interpretative, reporting, labelling.
            No . . . it's mine, I'm holding it.
            Relational, self-maintaining, self-emphasis.

2 *Sally*:   Let me look . . . I can too . . . it's not yours really.
            Relational, self-maintaining, justification.
            Yes I can see it there. (Tom lets Sally hold the snowstorm)
            Relational, self-maintaining, self-emphasis.

3 *Tom*:   I can see a little Christmas tree.
            Interpretative, reporting, detail.

4 *Sally*:   And I can see another funny man with a gun.
            Interpretative, reporting, detail.

5 *Tom*:   Watch when I shake it. (He shakes the object vigorously)
            Relational, self-maintaining, self-emphasis.

6 *Sally*:   Now what's happened . . . it's see-sawing.
            Interpretative, reporting, labelling.

7 *Tom*:   Yes it is and it's all going back to the ground. (This seems to refer to the snow which is settling)
            Interpretative, reporting, detail.

8 *Sally*:   (Points to a crack on the base). See it's got broken a little bit, hasn't it?
            Interpretative, reporting, detail.

9 *Tom*:   Somebody must have dropped it I think.
            Interpretative, reasoning, possible cause.
            (Tom puts down the snowstorm and both children turn back to look in the box)

10 *Sally*: And I've got one like this . . . at my house . . . but it isn't like this one . . .
            Interpretative, reporting, comparison.
            it's not got a see-saw in it . . . it's got a house in . . . with a man and a lady at the door . . . and the snow goes on them.
            Interpretative, reporting, detail.

11 *Tom*:   (Pulls elastic band from small box) I'm going to see what's in here . . .
            Directive, self-directing, monitoring action.

| 12 *Tom*: | (to Observer) Once I bringed home . . . those elastic bands at home . . . and I've left it at home now. |

Interpretative, reporting-recall, associated actions.

| *Observer*: | I see. |
| 13 *Tom*: | Sometimes I put one of those elastic bands in my gun . . . and it shoots everything. |

Interpretative, reporting-recall, associated actions.

| 14 *Sally*: | I'm giving this old lady a ride. |

Projective, imaginative, monitoring action.

(Sally has put the doll into a car and is pushing it round)

| 15 *Tom*: | I am getting the lorry now. And I'm putting this brick on. |

Directive, self-directing, monitoring action.

(Tom pulls out the small blocks and piles them on the lorry)

| 16 | This has got a very heavy load. |

Interpretative, reporting detail.

| 17 *Sally*: | Now he's going back home. |

Projective, imaginative, representing events.

(Sally bangs the car into a box and the doll falls off)

Oh . . . he's had an accident.

Projective, imaginative, representing events.

(She picks up the doll, puts it on the car and pushes it around the table)

| 18 | Come on . . . let me come through. |

Projective, imaginative, language of role.

That's a hospital now.

(She is referring to an upturned box)

Projective, imaginative, renaming.

It's a hospital.

Projective, imaginative, renaming.

| 19 *Tom*: | Get an ambulance . . . you've got to get an ambulance if you have an accident. |

Projective, imaginative, principle.

| 20 *Sally*: | And a doctor . . . doctors make people better. |

Projective, imaginative, principle.

(She pushes the doll over to the bed and puts it in)

| 21 | I'm going to get a doctor . . . |

Projective, imaginative, language of role.

He's getting better now.

Projective, imaginative, representing events.

| 22 | He's having a prick thing to make him better. |

Projective, imaginative, representing events.

| 23 *Tom*: | (to Observer) I haven't bringed a hanky with me. |

Relational, self-maintaining, absence of conditions.

Observer:		Here you are . . . here's one for you.
24	*Tom:*	I can't wipe my own nose.
		Relational, self-maintaining, absence of conditions.
Observer:		You can't? Let me help you.
25	*Sally:*	(to Observer) Shall I tell you something?
		Relational, self-maintaining, self-emphasis.
		I've got a sister called Helen
		Interpretative, reporting, detail.
		and she keeps saying very naughty things and do you know, Mummy tells her not to do it . . .
		Interpretative, reporting, detail.
		And I don't do *that* all the time.
		Relational, self-maintaining, self-emphasis.
Observer:		Don't you?
26	*Sally:*	Only sometimes.
		Relational, self-maintaining, self-emphasis.
27	*Tom:*	(Pushing a lorry over the policeman) Well I'm going to be very cross because the lorry ran over him.
		Projective, imaginative, representing events.
28		We'll have to bury the poor policeman now.
		Projective, imaginative, representing events.
29	*Sally:*	(Putting a doll into bed) This is the baby and she went into bed and then she went poorly.
		Projective, imaginative, representing events.
30	*Tom:*	And I'm getting something to put him in and he's going to be dead.
		Projective, imaginative, representing events.
31	*Sally:*	And she might have got a measles . . .
		Projective, imaginative, representing events.
		and I had measles and then Helen did . . . but we're better now.
		Interpretative, reporting-recall, sequence.
32	*Tom:*	(to Observer) My daddy will be coming soon and then I'm going home with him.
		Projective, predictive, forecasting.
Observer:		That's good.
33	*Tom:*	He's bringing me my coat 'cos I forgot it.
		Projective, predictive, causal relationship.
Observer:		Did you?
34	*Tom:*	It's in the car. I forgot to put it on so he'll bring it 'cos it's got thick fur inside to keep me warm.
		Projective, predictive, causal relationship.
Observer:		You are lucky aren't you?

35 *Tom*:   And then we're going to the shops . . . we might . . .
             and I might get a car . . . or a transporter . . .
             if my dad says so.
             Projective, predictive, possibilities.
36   And I might get some elastic bands for my gun . . .
             'cos I need some. But my dad might bring some home
             from work.
             Projective, predictive, possibilities.

The above extract is about one-tenth of the talk that Tom and Sally produced in the recording session of one hour. There were few problems in making a transcription of this section, there was little overlap of voices, no inaudible passages, or difficulties in picking up what the children said. Tom had some slight problems of articulation but none that hindered transcriptions being made.

In examining this extract we shall make some points about the uses of language that appeared regularly in the talk of the children in the advanted groups, but that were less frequent in or absent from the talk of the children in the disadvantaged groups.

All the children at some point used language that served the self-maintaining function. Tom and Sally each try to take possession of the snowstorm novelty at the beginning of the extract but Sally offers justification for her action as she reminds Tom that 'it's not yours really'. This argument is perhaps based on a general principle which they both know, that is, that both children have equal rights to an object that does not belong to either of them. There were several instances that demonstrated that these 3-year-olds were adopting basic commonly accepted principles to guide their behaviour. Knowing the principle did not necessarily mean that they could apply it, for sometimes their frustration or desire was too much for them. Nevertheless they were beginning to quote simple principles as a basis from which to justify their own behaviour or criticise the behaviour of others.

Several of the utterances that follow serve the interpretative function as the children report on what they see, with some reference to detail.

Tom at (9) offers a possible *cause* of the crack, which means that he is not only examining the detail of his experiences, but his efforts of interpretation include looking for explanations for what he sees. Sally at (10) begins to talk about past experiences, things not present in the immediate concrete situation. The children in the advantaged groups frequently began to talk spontaneously about things which lay outside the present situation. Often it was possible to see the object or action that had served to associate past experience with the present. In this case it is the snowstorm. Sally remembers the one she has at home and, as it were, makes an analysis of the contents in order to show how it is different. We might consider this orientation to be very important for the child's education, since we ask the child frequently to recall and to use information and experience that he has met in the past, and that is needed for the further interpretation of something happening in the present. The general inclination to make an analysis of experiences seems to be an orientation that will aid recall and the active use of past experiences.

Tom at (11), (12) and (13) exhibits very similar behaviour as he recalls his gun at home. Following this we see the children directing and monitoring their own actions, almost as though they are telling themselves what they are doing at (14), (15) and (16). It is perhaps worth noting the tendency of the advantaged child to label objects within the concrete present rather than to use pronouns that would have served adequately for communicating with one another.

At (17) Sally begins to project through the imagination, building up a situation that depends on words for its existence. Yet Tom, at (19), responds to Sally's words as though they are the reality and follows with a statement of a basic principle.

Sally pursues her imagined scene still further, spelling out imagined conditions and actions in her talk at (20), (21) and (22).

The use of language in this way for representing the imagined scene and action was a characteristic feature of the play and talk of all the 3-year-olds in the advantaged groups and was one of the main features which distinguished them from the disadvantaged groups.

At (23) and (24) we see Tom seeking help for himself – not by requests or demands but by making a statement of the situation. These utterances are classified as self-maintaining. At (25) Sally recalls her mother's talk about her sister's misbehaviour, before she returns to her imaginative play. This is classified as belonging to the interpretative function; the language use is reporting on past experience, and the strategies used are giving detail and making comparisons (25). The last utterance here, 'And I don't do that all the time', is clearly self-maintaining and is classified as such.

At this point, perhaps we can see behaviour like that described by Piaget as monologue, where the children seem to pursue their own thoughts in parallel. They are talking for themselves and pursuing separate topics without, it would seem, listening to each other.

27 *Tom*:   Well, I'm going to be very cross because the lorry ran over him.

29 *Sally*:   This is the baby and she went into bed and then she went poorly.

Because the children are injecting information about the scene they are imagining, they tend towards explicitness and avoid, it would seem, the use of pronouns. In imaginative play there must be considerable explicitness if others are to know what objects and actions represent.

At (32), (33) and (34), Tom is using language to talk about a remembered experience; he gives essential detail and a reasoned explanation, as he explains about leaving his coat in the car. This would be classified as belonging to the projective function and the language use is reasoning. At (35) he projects into the not too distant future and, as it were, surveys alternative possibilities. Such uses of language are evidence of the projective function, the predictive use of language and the strategy is surveying alternative possibilities. There are few examples of such uses of language, even in the talk of the 3-year-olds in the advantaged groups.

The above excerpts have been used to indicate both the kind of data which we had obtained and the problems of using the classification. There were few problems when deciding to which function utterances should be allocated, and the application of the general rule by which utterances were allocated to the use of language, or to the strategy, that was judged to be the most complex of those identified within the utterance, resolved most difficulties. (The numbering in the excerpts above is to aid reference: not all the utterances have been given a number.)

Perhaps the most difficult problem was in dealing with those utterances that might be judged as self-maintaining but in which other functions were realised. Utterances like the following example posed problems:

> Give me my car now 'cos it's nearly time for me to go home and my mum'll be cross if I don't take it home.

This utterance is clearly concerned with the child's own possessions and right. Therefore it is self-maintaining, and using a strategy of justification. However, at the same time it expresses a particular kind of interpretation of the child's problem by projecting into the consequences and the effects on other people. It might therefore be judged to be within the empathetic use of language or the predictive use. Since we considered the aspect of forecasting possible consequences to be the most complex of the strategies used this utterance was allocated to the projective function, the predictive use of language and to the strategy of forecasting possible consequences. Making decisions of this kind could distort the view gained of children's use of self-maintaining language, but there were so few instances in the talk of 3-year-olds that it is not the case in the present study.

The Results of the Functional Analysis

The comparison of the purposes for which the groups of children in the study used language was based on the numbers of utterances that had been allocated to the categories within the classification. A final adjustment was made to the scores so that they were based proportionately on the highest number of utterances produced by any group. It does not seem feasible to reproduce all the detail of the analysis here, but a summary of the major distinctions revealed by the analysis is given in Table 5 in the Appendix, page 190.

It had been recognised from the beginning that there were problems in making analyses of this kind. Although the criteria for making judgements seemed clear, it was anticipated that subjectivity might enter into decisions. It was therefore decided to ask an independent member to examine a one-tenth random sample of the scripts, after having discussed and practised making the judgements with the author. The correlation between the judgement of the two members was 0·9 overall and at a level between 0·8 and 0·99 on particular categories.

From an examination of the summary of the analysis, the following points can be made.

1   The disadvantaged groups of children used speech two and a half times as often as the advantaged groups to secure attention to their own needs and to maintain their own status by defending or asserting themselves in the face of the needs and actions of others.
2   The advantaged groups used language more than five times as often as the less favoured groups for extending or promoting action, and for securing collaboration with others: language is seen to play a directing or controlling role more frequently. The disadvantaged groups used language more often as part of, or as a support to, ongoing action: language tended to accompany action rather than to control or direct it.
3   The advantaged groups used language almost eight times as often to refer to past experiences and more than twice as often to contemplate the future.
4   The advantaged groups used language more than nine times as frequently for reasoning – in real or imagined contexts. The advantaged groups used more than twice as much speech for projection through the imagination as the disadvantaged groups, and more than five times as much for projecting beyond the use of concrete materials for creating an imagined situation.
5   We attempted to distinguish between language that seemed to require no listener other than the self and that addressed to other children or to the adult. The disadvantaged groups used slightly more speech that appeared to be only for the self than the advantaged groups (17 and 13·6 per cent of all speech respectively). The advantaged groups, on the other hand, addressed the adult more frequently than the disadvantaged groups (30·0 and 19·9 per cent of all utterances respectively). There were differences here between the nursery and the non-nursery groups.

The advantaged non-nursery group addressed the adult almost twice as often as the nursery advantaged group (41·2 and 21·1 per cent of all utterances) and, contrary to expectations, the disadvantaged non-nursery group addressed the adult more frequently than the disadvantaged nursery group (23·0 and 15·6 per cent of all utterances).

The Analysis of the Children's Questions

Finally all the questions asked by the children during the recording sessions were analysed.

An examination of the structural features of the questions asked revealed little difference between the groups except in the use of 'why?', which in any case appeared rarely and was used only by a few children in the advantaged groups.

The second approach considered the functions that the questions served. Again the differences between the groups were not great, but this analysis does seem to offer some indications of the kind of interest and awareness that the 3-year-old was demonstrating through his questioning behaviour. The classification is a crude one and is seen as no more than exploratory.

The following, then, were the categories recognised.

1 Questions which appeared to serve self needs (both physical and psychological needs), that is, they were self-maintaining.
   e.g. Have you got some sweets for me? Will you watch me?
   Included in this group of questions were those that sought permission for some action by the child.
   e.g. Can I go too?
2 A second group of questions, closely related to the first group, contained those that were concerned with the views and feelings of others. Included in the category were:
   (a) Tags which aimed at establishing rapport.
       e.g. Shall we? Do you know?
   (b) Those questions concerned with the assets or abilities of others.
       e.g. Is that car yours? Can you jump as high as me?
   (c) Questions concerned with the feelings or needs of others.
       e.g. Are you mad about that? Do you want a sweet?
   (d) Questions concerned with the opinions or actions of others.
       e.g. Do you like my red sandals? Are you going to keep it?
   (e) Questions which drew attention to the speaker.
       e.g. Can you see what I'm doing? Are you watching me?
   The majority of these questions would also be judged as self-maintaining.

3 This group of questions seemed to be aimed at gaining some kind of direction or instruction, and it might be considered to lie within the directive function:
   (a) for ending doubt,
       e.g. Have I to cut it now?
   (b) for an instruction 'how' or 'when',
       e.g. How does this fasten? When do I turn it?
   (c) for an instruction about a course of action,
       e.g. What have I to do next?
4 This category included all those questions that sought for the identification of some object, person, action, place or time. More than half the questions from all the groups of children fell into this category. They could be seen as serving the interpretative function.
   e.g. What's that? Who's the lady? Where's my car?
5 This covered a small group of questions that were judged as seeking for knowledge, either by way of description or through explanation, and might be judged as serving the interpretative function at a more complex level.
   e.g. What's this springy thing for? How did that fire engine get brokened? Why is she going out?
6 Another small set of questions appeared in some way to be projective, that is, they related to situations that were not present, or not obvious, at the time of asking. These questions anticipated events, or recalled events, or were concerned with possibilities or other dependency relationships, and clearly were evidence of the projective function of language.
   e.g. Might you come again next week? If you don't want it can I take it home? Will that fall down when she puts that brick on top? Is it the same as last time?
   Also included in this category were questions that served to promote the imagined situation.
   e.g. Will she get better, doctor?
7 Finally, there were check tags, e.g. isn't it? doesn't she? don't you? can't I?
   These were attachments to statements that have been analysed along with the utterances that were not questions.

SUMMARY OF RESULTS OF THE ANALYSIS OF QUESTIONS

The following points can be drawn from the analysis of the children's questions.
1 Contrary to what might have been expected, the total number of questions asked by the disadvantaged group exceeds that of the

advantaged groups. The disadvantaged nursery group asked almost twice as many questions as any of the other three groups.

2 The advantaged non-nursery group showed more concern for their own particular needs than the other groups, although it should be noted that this is based on the proportion of the questions asked and not on the actual number of questions asked. A greater proportion of questions put by the advantaged groups that fell within this category were for seeking permission than for other needs. The disadvantaged groups, and particularly the non-nursery group, are seen to be more concerned with others: these questions can be seen generally to relate to the defence of the child's own position in relation to others.

3 All the children in all the groups used a large number of questions simply for the purpose of establishing the identity of objects. 'What's this (or that)?' occurs frequently amongst the questions of all the children in these groups.

4 A greater proportion of the questions asked by the advantaged non-nursery group were seeking for some instruction or direction. This reflects perhaps their relative insecurity in this kind of play situation, since they turned more frequently to the adult for reassurance. Again it must be pointed out that this relates to the proportion of the questions asked and not to the actual number of questions.

5 The only clear difference between the advantaged and the disadvantaged groups is in the number and proportion of questions that sought for explanations. Such questions were in any case infrequent: twenty-eight were put by the advantaged groups and six by the disadvantaged groups.

6 It can be seen that in the category described as 'projective' there are very few questions that anticipate, or predict, or consider the feelings of others. The few questions of this kind that do appear are all put by children in the advantaged groups.

SOME DIFFERENCES IN THE USE OF LANGUAGE: A DISCUSSION OF THE RESULTS

Whilst this analysis of the functions and uses of children's language clearly presents many difficulties, and cannot be as objective as those analyses that examine linguistic features, nevertheless it serves to raise questions about what might be important differences in orientation between the advantaged and the disadvantaged groups. Already by the age of 3 years, language seems to be playing an important part in directing the child's attention or search within the immediate situation: from the results of the analysis it would seem that the advantaged child may be more closely in control of his own actions and have established a greater alertness for anticipating the possibilities for action than the disadvantaged child.

As has been seen from other analyses, the child from the advantaged group is more likely to use speech to project beyond the limits of the immediate situation. Children from the advantaged groups are seen to use language a great deal more than the disadvantaged groups for imaginative projection, particularly in the creation and extension of imagined situations that go beyond the interpretation of concrete materials. The possibility that this self-imposed exercise may bring an important extension of the projective function, which may promote particular kinds of skills in thinking, must be considered.

To what extent might differences in the conditions present have influenced children's behaviour and use of language in play and account for the observed differences? Whilst it is true that it is difficult to make every play session identical, and therefore to provide exactly the same opportunity for certain kinds of skill to be displayed, an examination of the records suggests that whilst there are differences for individual children the variation seems to affect all groups to about the same extent. The choice of companion may influence the kind of play which develops: this may particularly affect the readiness with which imaginative play is developed. Joan, for example, follows the lead of Jane, and so may use more language in this kind of situation than she would had she chosen a less dominant companion. In spite of this she uses little speech to extend the imaginative situation, even though her more favoured companion continually demonstrates its use for this purpose.

The choice of companion may also influence the extent to which the adult is drawn into participation, or must intervene for some reason, and this may affect the child's responses. Whilst the same materials were always used by the children it was still true that the play situation took place in different surroundings. As far as could be seen, however, these differences had not contributed in any major way to the recordings.

The analyses based on the classification described in Chapters 5 and 6 have indicated that differences in the use of language do exist between these selected groups of children. Although we have recognised from the outset that there were problems of design in the project and every effort was made to meet them at each point, it is difficult to judge to what extent they have been overcome or avoided.

Whilst it is true that the selection procedures did not provide a group of children from the most disadvantaged section of the population (that is most disadvantaged with respect to education), they did in fact provide groups that are distinguished by differences in the fostering practices within the home that seem likely to influence the child's learning and use of language skills (Tough and Sestini, in preparation).

The feature that is most open to criticism is the language sampling situation. In spite of all efforts to present the same conditions to all children, it was impossible to control all aspects of the situation. There were differences in the physical surroundings; rooms in schools and rooms in houses differ in their general content. Such differences seem to introduce differences in vocabulary rather than in structure or function of language, however.

The temperament of the child and the effect of this on his response to the situation had been considered, and only friendly and co-operative children had been sought and found. In spite of this, a few children were a little shy in the recording session, particularly at the beginning. The advantaged non-nursery group contained most of these children. This might be expected to affect the language samples: in fact it seems mainly to affect the number of utterances recorded, since on the several measures their performance lies within the range of the rest of the group.

Choice of playmate also provided a hazard that was difficult to avoid. Generally the pairs of children played readily together, but it is possible that the readiness with which the child embarked on imaginative play might be affected by the responses of the second child. Care was taken to offer the same kind of invitation to all children to use the materials for imaginative play but in fact there were wide differences in the amount of language used by individual children in imaginative play within all groups. There is, however, no evidence to suggest that the use of imaginative play results in differences in the other aspects measured.

Although the language sampling situation is open to such criticism, as far as can be seen there is no gross distortion of the results because of these recognised hazards. The aspects on which differences have been identified were demonstrated consistently by members of the groups, and only one child from the disadvantaged group on some measures had scores that were better than the scores of one or two children in the advantaged group.

To the alerted listener there were obvious differences in the language used by children from different social environments. What is not so clearly evident is the extent to which these differences in language might be the expression of a range of differences that exist between children in their cognitive dealings with experience.

The views taken of the world around them by the children in the advantaged and disadvantaged groups seemed to differ in the awareness they showed of the qualities of their experiences. The disadvantaged child showed more concern for his status and issued instructions to others that were aimed at maintaining his status; he more frequently showed concern for his possessions and demanded consideration of his particular needs.

Much of the language of the child in a disadvantaged group appeared as a way of monitoring the ongoing situation in order to be alert to any threat to his position, or was directed towards the successful maintenance of his position in relation to others. It is of course true that children in the advantaged groups used language for the same purpose but to a lesser

4

extent: the alertness to the ongoing situation that they showed was revealed in the attention that they gave to the detail of the environment, and in expressing awareness of qualitative aspects of their experiences and in the recognition of relationships.

The main characteristic of the language of the advantaged group that distinguished them from the disadvantaged group, however, was the ease with which they projected in their thinking beyond the ongoing situation to recall and re-savour past experiences, to anticipate and examine possible future experiences and to create, as it were, new experiences for themselves through the imagination. The children in the disadvantaged groups showed little inclination to manipulate their experiences in any way except in the direction of maintaining their own status, but those in the advantaged groups expressed through their language an inclination to seek for explanations and for associations and to survey the range of possibilities which were open to them.

So we can see that through the language children are using it becomes evident that there is a difference in the range of phenomena which they recognise, or at least find it important to refer to. But it is also clear that language is providing a vehicle for the expression of the child's focus of attention at any particular point. When Mandy says 'When I get home my daddy's going to put up a new – a blue kind of swing thing – in the garden, he is, if he's home in time' she is not giving her fully focused attention to the form of what she is saying, that is, to the speech itself; but rather is she focusing on the information she wants to give, the meaning she is trying to convey, that is, she is concerned with the purpose of using language. It is also true that at certain points she switches her attention to the form the language needs to take because she becomes aware that her intended meaning has not been successfully expressed through the speech she has used.

This too is a characteristic of the talk of the advantaged child: the flow of talk as an idea is expressed, the hesitation as attention swings to the speech, the restatement, the qualifying phrase, the restart. This phenomenon (referred to by Bernstein, 1958, Goldman-Eisler, 1968, and others) perhaps is an indication of the relationships that exist between the speech form, that is the structures used, and the function which the language fulfils. The child struggles for the adequate expression of meaning and speech structures are pressed into serving the function. The more complex the meaning, the more frequently does the child's attention need to be diverted to secure the structures that will allow its expression.

In our recordings of children's talk we have many examples to show that the meaning that the child intended to express was not met by a knowledge of, or ready access to, suitable structures for its expression. In these instances the child pressed into use expressions that seemed to hold the meaning nicely but that might not be recognised as 'well formed', for example 'coming big soon' to mean growing bigger or older, and 'might it was grandma' for 'perhaps it was grandma'.

From the analysis of the uses of language it became clear that there were differences between the advantaged and the disadvantaged groups of 3-year-olds in the kinds of meanings that they were imposing on their experiences and that were expressed through language. Although the children in the disadvantaged groups used language at least as much as the advantaged groups, their language tended to be limited to the ongoing present experience and to monitoring their own activities. The children in the disadvantaged groups used language much less frequently than the children in the advantaged groups for:

1 analysing and reasoning about present and past experiences, and recognising overall structure;
2 projecting beyond the present experience to future events, possible alternative courses and consequences, and into the feelings and experiences of others;
3 creating imagined scenes for their play which were dependent on the use of language for their existence for others.

It would seem from this that there is justification for stating that these 3-year-old children, coming from different home environments, had established different priorities for expressing meaning, and different orientations towards the use of language.

PART II

Chapter 8

Sampling the Language Used at 5 and 7 Years Old

In several ways the analysis of the language of the groups of 3-year-olds produced unexpected results. Perhaps the least expected result was to find that 3-year-olds could already be so competent in the use of language. This was something of a surprise, since there could have been little more than a year, or a year and a half, for the development from the typical 2-year-old telegraphic speech to take place. Now, many of the children in the selected groups were using complex structures frequently, with only minor errors occurring but, more surprisingly, some were using language that reflected quite complex thinking. It is clear, however, that not all children at the age of 3 have developed the same skills, and the differences between the language of the advantaged and the disadvantaged groups was evidence of this.

The objectives for the further study of the language of these same children was to try to trace the development that was taking place as they grew older, and to discover whether the differences between the groups remained, and whether they would become more extensive.

Perhaps the most difficult problem to solve in studying language in use is to decide the kind of situation in which data should be collected. Where there is interest in language used in particular kinds of context the problem is reduced, except that there is then a temptation to generalise from one kind of context to all contexts. The problem in trying to follow the developing skill of children is to decide what might be considered to be a fully representative sample of the child's overall use of language.

In selecting a play situation in which to collect the language used by 3-year-olds, we had recognised that although this may not produce examples of all that he can do with language, nevertheless play is a major occupation of the 3-year-old, and whether it is structured deliberately by offering particular materials to him, or whether he is responding spontaneously to the objects that come into his path, he is likely to settle happily and talk readily about what he is doing. The child plays not only because toys and play materials, for example sand and water, are provided for him, but also because any object may precipitate some interest, and stimulate imagination and perhaps also some symbolic activity. Play is a particular kind of response that is characteristic of the young child, and as he plays he may be expected to talk out loud to himself, and to others who may be near. His play seems to provide him with an opportunity to practise much that he is learning about language in other contexts, just as he practises his growing control of movement as he enjoys physical play.

Although the play situation devised for the collection of data at the 3-year-old stage may not have sampled everything that the child could do with language, it seemed likely to produce much of what he could do with language. As he played with his chosen friend, in the presence of an accepted adult, it seemed likely that he would use familiar ways of relating to children and adults, and that his language would reflect his typical orientation towards the use of language.

At the age of 3 years, clearly the child's immaturity will be a major factor in determining the view he is able to take of a particular situation. He is likely to employ the kinds of strategies that he is already familiar with and would use in other similar situations. For example, in symbolic play in which the child imitates the behaviour of familiar people, particularly the mother, he is likely to produce the patterns of speech that are being absorbed into his own pattern of responses. Jane, for example, as she plays with her doll, reveals both in the verbal pattern, and in the intonation pattern, strategies that form a basis for addressing others when she responds to them in reality.

She picks up the toy telephone and says:

Jane:	Hello, is that you doctor?
Jane:	(replying for the doctor) Yes.
Jane:	Doctor . . . my baby is poorly.
	(She turns to the doll) You *are* poorly.
Observer:	Are you talking to the doctor?
Jane:	I'm going to ask him . . .
	(She speaks into the telephone)
	25543 . . . Who's that speaking? The doctor?
	My baby is poorly . . . so make it better . . .
	come along quickly. Good . . . quickly.
Observer:	What did the doctor say?
Jane:	Yes, I will . . . that's what the doctor said.
	This baby's poorly.
Observer:	Oh dear.
Jane:	Yes . . . it had some . . . it had some . . . it had some
	things like that . . . it had some measles.

In this short extract we can see that Jane already has expectations about interaction. She plays the several parts, including the baby and the doctor, as well as relating in reality to the observer. She clearly knows the purpose of questions and is familiar with ways of responding.

At the age of 3, children are not deliberately planning their behaviour, they are not generally mature enough to be projecting into the position of the listener and modifying their own behaviour with the perspective of other people in mind, nor do they have an awareness of the different kinds of relationships they are engaging in. They respond with strategies with which they have been made familiar in their interaction with others. Sometimes it must be that these familiar strategies are no more than phrases that 'belong' to a particular kind of situation. The meaning may be a global one, and does not necessarily indicate specific understanding of each word used.

For example, Janet is playing with a doll in a bath.

Janet: Look she's sitting on the bath with bare feet and she fell off . . . see . . . she fell in the bath upside down . . . see . . . that's very unfortunate.
Janet picks up the doll.
        There you're all right again.

In this example Janet is clearly reproducing phrases she has heard used in the 'bath time' context. The phrases are meaningful in this context but 'bare' may not be a generalised meaning and 'unfortunate' is hardly likely to be. Nevertheless, they are used appropriately within this context and this, perhaps, brings them within the possibility of understanding and of generalising meaning.

In re-examining the play situation that was used for the collection of data when the children were 3, there is ample evidence to show that this did provide a situation in which the 3-year-old produced a wide range of complex structures and a wide range of uses. It is difficult to know what other kinds of context might have provided a more suitable and productive situation for the collection of children's talk.

At the ages of $5\frac{1}{2}$ and $7\frac{1}{2}$, however, it was argued that a play situation seemed unlikely to provide a view of all that the child could now do with language. Because of the child's greater maturity and experience of using language, he has built up well-established attitudes to using language in different contexts. This is not to say that some children might not display a general orientation to use language in similar ways, whatever the context, but it might be important that some children do in fact have quite different expectations from context to context and only in some contexts do their expectations lead them to certain uses of language.

One of the most difficult problems to resolve at this stage of the project was to decide on those situations that seemed most likely to provide representative samples of the child's language. The major criticism that can be made of language tests is that although they provide objective data of what is done in response to the test situation, this may be very untypical of other situations in which the individual uses language. But this criticism can also be levelled at studies that use one kind of context only in which to record a sample of the child's language.

It was clear that we could not attempt to sample the child's language in the whole range of different situations in which he uses language. The main aim of the project was to examine whether the differences that were found to be developing at the age of 3 seemed likely to be contributing to the child's relative advantage or disadvantage in school.

It seemed essential, then, to sample the child's language in situations that would reveal the kind of responses he could make to 'educational' contexts and to examine uses of language upon which learning might be dependent.

We agree that there are many other variables, besides the child's ability in using language, that affect what the child will learn in school. For example, the view the teacher has of the child, and the assumptions and values that the teacher holds, will affect the relationship that is set up between teacher and child. The child's personality and adjustment to the classroom also seem likely to play an important part, as does the availability of suitable 'concrete' experiences.

In selecting situations that reflected what might be referred to as the 'educational strategies' that children were likely to meet in school, we also had in mind that they should between them sample the range of uses of language that seemed to be the essential basis from which education should proceed. We will not justify this approach at this point. We are aware that our assumptions in this matter reflect a view of what the aims of education in early childhood ought to be and we shall return to discuss this matter in a later chapter.

A structured interview technique was used in which materials, which were expected to be of interest to the child, were presented and a series of questions was asked, with a number of permitted probes following each to encourage the reticent child and help the restless child to focus his attention on the problem in hand.

It was expected that the child's responses in such task-oriented situations would not necessarily reflect his habitual use of language in peer group interaction. Therefore it was planned to include two opportunities to record the child talking as he played with his friend with some of the materials.

These recordings provided approximately one hour's talk at the age of 5 years and an hour and a half's talk at the age of 7. In both cases a natural break in the interview sequence was provided.

All the children in the groups responded willingly to these interviews and generally talked readily. There was a general feeling of interest and all seemed well motivated to take part in the work. Since contact between home and the observer had been maintained since the child was 3, the observer was greeted as an old friend and the children appeared to be happy at being asked to accompany the observer and talk and work with her.

When the children were traced at the age of $5\frac{1}{2}$ several children had moved, but only three children were found to have moved such a distance that they could not be followed up. Their places were filled by the nearest match from the extended group on their performance at the age of 3. At the age of 7 one of the children who had not been available at the age of 5 had returned; others had moved, but only two had moved so far away that it was not possible to follow them up. Again it was possible to fill their places from the extended group, so that all through the study subgroups of twelve children were maintained.

Although seven different situations were devised for sampling children's language at the ages of $5\frac{1}{2}$ and $7\frac{1}{2}$ years, it became clear when results were analysed that some of the situations had produced very similar results and drawn upon the same skills in using language. For this reason, we are drawing on only three of the situations used at the age of $5\frac{1}{2}$, and six of the situations used at the age of $7\frac{1}{2}$. Each situation will be described at a relevant point in the text. All the data were subjected to two kinds of analysis: an analysis of the linguistic structures using the same methods as in the analysis of the data from the 3-year-olds, and an analysis of the uses of language.

The tasks used for these later stages of the project, then, were devised so that they would evoke particular uses of language, those that it seemed would be needed, and expected by teachers, in response to the activities provided in school as a basis for learning.

It was expected that the interpretative function of language would be frequently drawn upon in school, thus tasks were designed so that the *reporting* and *reasoning* uses of language would be stimulated. The analyses distinguished the strategies of reporting and reasoning in the children's responses. Explorations of the development of the interpretative function of language are found in Chapters 9, 10, 11 and 12.

The projective function, revealed as we have seen in the use of language for predicting and imagining, is frequently called upon and the child is expected to use language for these purposes and to respond to language used by the teacher for these purposes. The responses children gave to an activity that depended upon language used in this way are discussed in Chapter 10. The childs' ability to use language for directing other people was also considered and is reported in Chapter 13.

The tasks generally fulfilled their purpose, that is, the language used by the children in response to the tasks was generally of the kind intended. Responses were analysed on the basis of the strategies of language used by the child and answers were then classified according to the most complex strategies that appeared in the response. For example, if this part of a child's response was at the level of *labelling* and the remainder was at the level of *central meaning*, the child's answer was classified as *central meaning* and the more complex thinking was recognised.

Chapter 9

Interpreting Experiences

What kind of meanings do children place on their everyday experiences? Is it the case that meanings are developing differently and that children will make interpretations of experiences that are consistently different from those made by others? In earlier chapters we have quoted the works of Sapir, Whorf, Luria, Vygotsky and Bernstein to support the view that the language environment necessarily shapes the interpretation that children are likely to place upon their experiences. Are such differences of interpretation likely to contribute anything to the child's ability to respond to, and benefit from, his experiences in school?

Questions like these were emerging as the second part of the longitudinal study was approached. We had seen that at 3 years of age the children in the groups described as advantaged and disadvantaged already tended to show differences in orientation towards the use of language, and these differences were made clear by the kinds of meanings that it seemed they found appropriate to express during their spontaneous play. The tendency towards different interpretations had been shown, for example, in the extent to which children referred to past experience, drawing it into the present, and by so doing, it seemed, extending the meaning of the present situation. Differences also had been found in the frequency with which children looked ahead and planned their activities or anticipated events that might take place in the future.

A first approach to the examination of these questions was to discover how the children would respond to pictures of familiar scenes. Although it might be argued that pictures cannot be compared with ongoing experiences, the difficulties of trying to create the same ongoing situation for sixty-four children in a number of schools seemed insurmountable. But pictures are a familiar means of presenting information to children, and we expect quite young children to be able to interpret pictures as though they were ongoing situations. After considering the results of this investigation, it would seem that such assumptions may not be justified.

In deciding to use pictures, it seemed important that any picture used should draw on experiences that were equally familiar to all children, and that the pictures should have embodied in them a meaning that required the child to make some analysis in order to place an overall interpretation on it.

At the age of 5, the scene presented to the children consisted of a group of people in a room. A girl was standing with her hands in the sink, a woman was standing nearby with her arm outstretched towards the girl and looking down at her, a man was sitting at the table, holding a news-paper as though reading it, and a boy was standing beside a chest of drawers, with his hands outstretched towards a cat, which was sitting on the top of the chest.

This scene had been put together in a box to form a peepshow. It had the qualities of a three-dimensional picture and had been designed to arouse the child's interest at 'peeping' into the room, but also to make clear to the child the need for explicitness, because the interviewer did not have his view of what was happening, and to discourage him from pointing instead of talking.

We had visited all the homes of the children and felt that the room depicted was one with which every child in the group would be able to identify. We expected that all the children would see the figures as people, and recognise their activities. The only bias towards 'class' characteristics might have been the presence of a newspaper, but no child in any group had difficulty in recognising it as a newspaper. Some children did not have cats in their homes, but nevertheless none appeared to have difficulty in identifying it, except one who referred to it as a 'little dog'.

The same question was put to all the children after inviting them to have a good look at the peepshow. 'Tell me all about what's happening in there, will you?' and the child's response was received with supportive nods, and comments. When the child appeared to have finished what he intended to say, he was prompted twice with 'Anything else?', 'Can you tell me anything more?' If the child's first response was, in effect, a synthesis of the whole, for example 'It's a family in the kitchen', the following comment asked the child to justify his interpretation: 'Why do you think that?'

All the children seemed to find the peepshow something of a novelty and all responded readily. Even when the 'picture' was enclosed, however, some found it difficult not to point: 'It's there at the back.' There were three different levels of response to this situation.

Some children replied as though they had been asked to make an inventory of the contents of the peepshow, listing some or all of the objects in the scene. The fullest description, for example, was this:

Tom: A lady and a mister, and there's a girl and a boy –
           and there's a cat as well.
Observer: Yes there is – can you tell me anything else about it?
Tom: Yes some things – drawers and the cat's on it and a table and
           a chair and the man's got a newspaper.

This approach seemed to be one of matching the contents of the peep-show with labels. It was as though the child let his eyes rest on one object after another, as he used language strategies of *labelling*.

A second type of response was also well represented. In this, objects were linked together, and the language strategies used were the *elaboration of detail* and *recognition of associated objects, actions and events*; for example:

Jimmy: There's a man reading a newspaper. The girl's got her hands in the sink . . . she's washing up. There's a boy and he's hitting the cat. And there's a lady.

This is clearly a different type of response from the first. The objects are linked by either actions or proximity. In this kind of response there is evidence of some structuring of the scene, although it still remains as though the child has examined each part of the scene in isolation from the rest, moving around the main figures in the room and then describing actions or positions.

A third type of response is clearly different again, in that there is an indication that the child realises that there is a coherence within the whole scene that is important. The elements, although existing in their own right, in some way relate to each other. There is an attempt to communicate this structure, or coherence, as the meaning to which all parts contribute, that is the language strategies used include the *recognition of central meaning*; for example:

Jill: Well . . . I think it must be a family in the kitchen . . . after breakfast.
Observer: I wonder why you think that.
Jill: Well . . . because . . . well . . . the little girl's washing up . . . I think . . . 'cos she's got her hands in the bowl hasn't she? And the daddy's sitting by the table and he's reading the newspaper, and my dad reads the newspaper at breakfast time.
Observer: Yes I see.
Jill: And I think the boy's just going to school cos he's got his coat on and he's saying 'Goodbye' to the cat. And the mummy's telling the little girl to hurry up. They're all in the kitchen after breakfast *I* think.

Some of the answers that were given, though not as full as Jill's, nevertheless indicated that the child saw the whole scene as a structure and uses a language strategy of *recognising a central meaning*; for example:

John: The mum's telling the children to go out to play and not to hurt the cat. And the dad's going to wait a bit.
Ian: The boy's telling the cat to get down off the sideboard and it's a family, getting ready to go out . . . 'cos she's washing her hands and the dad's not going.

What differences in the child's view of the situation do such responses reflect?

Looking at a picture is perhaps not so simple a task as we imagine. It implies that children can accept drawings (or models, in the case of the peepshow) as a representation of the real thing. None of the children indicated that he did not interpret the scene in the peepshow, and the pictures presented at the age of 7, as anything other than the scene it was supposed to represent.

But a picture, like the real situation it represents, is not just a number of objects, or a number of objects standing in some kind of relationship with one another. When we look at a picture, we try to look at the whole situation and see the central meaning towards which the parts of the situation contribute.

Perhaps we do not realise how much learning must take place before the child is able to interpret a picture in this way. Many children are introduced to pictures at an early age, certainly before they are able to talk much. Parents intuitively help the child to develop a way of scanning the picture, and when he has problems of interpreting the picture, they indicate the details that are important and help the child to give attention to them. In this way the child is learning over a long period how to set meanings on pictures, so that when he comes to school at the age of 5 he is able to make sense of what he sees in pictures.

For a full interpretation of the scene of the family in the peepshow, it was necessary to 'scan' the contents and look for relationships between the parts, and above all to look for any conflicts within the situation that must be resolved, or aspects that must be reconciled within any interpretation.

In the case of the peepshow, the child needed to scan the scene – centring attention on each figure and its activity – and then try to find an interpretation that would accommodate all that he saw. In fact, it is rather more complex than this. It means being open to possible interpretations of each person's part in the scene and being able to examine the possible alternative interpretations and select those that are compatible with an overall interpretation.

A child like Ian, who centres on one object and then moves from object to object, naming as he goes, 'A girl and a boy, a man and a lady' seems to fail to see that the scene is a composite whole. It is difficult to understand why his attention is not taken by the cat sitting up on top of the chest of drawers, for example, and why the outstretched arm of the boy does not challenge him to interpret the relationship that is suggested. If this reflects the way in which he views the world around him, then perhaps it would indicate that he lives in a world that has few relationships, little structure, and one in which all elements are separate and unrelated. Yet, if he were in a room like this, we would expect him to act with awareness of its structure and perhaps engage himself with the cat. But we may be making unjustified assumptions about his view of the picture. It is possible that the child makes an overall interpretation but still does not see the relevance of conveying the whole meaning to the interviewer. Perhaps he interprets the scene satisfactorily for himself but does not see that it is relevant to communicate his interpretation to other people. Yet no child seemed hostile and they all seemed intrigued by the peepshow. There was, then, no indication that they were not well motivated to respond.

All the responses given by the children to the first question and the following two prompts could be placed in one of the following three categories based on the strategies of language used:

1. listing or labelling;
2. connecting or associating objects, actions and events;
3. imposing a structure or looking for a central meaning.

There were differences between the advantaged and disadvantaged groups in the kind of interpretation used. Nineteen of the twenty-four children in the advantaged groups placed an overall interpretation on the scene and indicated the basis on which the interpretation was made. The remaining five used the 'associating' approach, dealing with each figure separately but making some interpretation about the actions or intentions: 'The boy's going to stroke the cat.'

In the disadvantaged groups, only four children placed any overall structure on the scene, six linked objects by actions or location, and fourteen responded by listing the people and objects in the room.

Are the differences in response of any importance? What differences might they reflect in the child's thinking? The overall structure, which many children in the advantaged groups placed on the scene, seem to spring from an orientation to treat the scene as a problem, in which the possible interpretations of each part of the scene must be, as it were, 'tested' against the next. Interpretations must be set upon the man's activity, the woman's activity and the actions of the boy and girl, and all must be reconciled to reach a possible explanation that encompasses the actions of all four figures in the scene.

When children come to school at 3 and at 5, we generally assume that pictures can be used to give information, but we should perhaps think again about our practice, for many children, it seems, may not be interpreting pictures at the level we expect.

The Interpretations of 7-Year-Olds

A second view of the child's ability to interpret a familiar scene given in picture form was taken when the children were $7\frac{1}{2}$. No child in any group was unfamiliar with a busy road with traffic and traffic lights, and the problems of crossing. Many of the children crossed such busy roads on their way to school and all lived within a short distance of a busy thoroughfare.

The picture presented to the children on this second occasion showed a boy stepping off the pavement on to the road and into the pathway of a bus, at a controlled crossing and with the traffic lights at green. The girl has her hand on the boy's arm and her face shows fear or extreme concern; a child on the opposite side of the road is waving, and the bus driver is looking down at the boy.

The same approach was used as at the earlier age. The child was asked to have a good look at the picture and then asked by the interviewer-researcher, 'Tell me all about what's happening here, will you?'

Again the groups were compared on the levels at which interpretations had been made. Several children in the advantaged groups scanned the scene and then offered an effective summary of the situation; for example, 'I think there's going to be an accident because this boy is just going to run across the road when the bus is coming'. Although it might seem at first glance that such summaries have neglected a great deal of information, the case is the opposite. To make such a summary a great deal of the data has to be recognised and reconciled to give an explanation that is compatible with all the data. The colour of the lights, the look on the girl's face, all give clues to the most likely overall meaning of the picture.

When children gave such overall summaries as their first response, they were asked to justify their judgements, so that it was possible to see what particular features of the picture they had taken into account. As before, two supportive prompts were offered to the children.

In organising the interpretation of the scene, three different strategies of language could be identified:

1　The different components of the scene were identified and labelled, that is, the language strategy was *labelling*, for example:
　　There's a boy and a girl and there's a bus, a red one, and some traffic lights.

In this kind of response, as we have already noted, it is as though the child moves the focus of his attention from one figure to the next, dealing with each separately, and giving a label for each person or object.

2　The second kind of response, as before, also identifies the components of the scene but there is some additional interpretation of the actions of the figure upon whom the child's attention is fixed; for example,
　　The boy's running on to the road and the girl's holding up her hand like this (demonstrates) and that boy's waving his hand.

The strategies of language used are *the elaboration of detail*, and the *association of objects, actions and events*.

3   The third kind of strategy is to place some interpretation upon the behaviour of the people in the scene, and the strategies include *recognition of central meaning*, recognising *causal and dependent relationships* and *forecasting possibilities or consequences*; for example:
> Well, there'll be an accident if that boy's not careful, because he's running on to the road and he hasn't seen that the lights are at 'go' and the bus is coming. The bus driver might be trying to stop but the girl thinks he won't be able to.

In making this kind of response, it is clear that the child is trying to project into the position of each of the participants in the scene. He is 'making sense' of what he sees and using his own knowledge of what happens in situations like this to account for the expressions on the faces of the girl and the bus driver.

By comparison the advantaged groups of children used twice as many utterances that are at this third level of interpretation as the disadvantaged group. The number of utterances that are at the second level of interpretation are about the same for the two groups, but the disadvantaged groups used almost twice as many utterances that are at the first level illustrated, of *labelling* the components in the scene.

Again it is difficult to accept that the disadvantaged child would behave differently in an actual situation of this kind. Indeed, it might be argued that many disadvantaged children living in city centres may display a great deal more competence in coping with the problem of crossing roads than would more advantaged children over whom a closer watch is exercised by parents. We cannot argue about this, since there is little evidence to show whether there are differences between groups in the way in which they would respond to actual situations of this kind. What can be said is that it is possible to 'know' a great deal about a situation in terms of the actions needed, and to operate on the basis of these without ever needing to express, either to oneself or to others, the basis on which actions are being pursued.

Thus, much of Piaget's evidence about children's thinking shows that the child can operate, and demonstrate by what he does, the basis of his thinking, without necessarily being able to be explicit in his explanations.

Or we might consider Bruner's three dimensions of knowing, and accept the possibility that knowledge can lie in the motor responses themselves or in the images that provide an internal model of the world on which actions can be performed, without necessarily being transformed into language (Bruner, 1964).

Such possibilities fit the facts of the observations we can make of ourselves as we operate; for example, as we judge the speed of oncoming traffic without necessarily ever becoming aware that we are doing so. Vygotsky makes the point that language arises at the point of becoming aware of operating in a particular way, of making judgements, of evaluating and of having intentions towards others. The very emergence of language, overtly or covertly, is evidence of the awareness of the self, and of the self's own actions and intentions.

The differences in children in the way in which they interpret situations may be, therefore, not so much evidence of differences in their interpretation of such scenes in terms of needed action, but rather of differences in their *awareness* of the fact that they are making judgements about actions.

When interpreting situations presented in pictures, the child is required to respond by projecting into all the elements of the scene and to take account of several viewpoints. It is possible that if the question had been 'What should the boy do now?' that some children might have found it easier to respond in terms of the boy's action because this would have related more directly to their own perceptions of the situation.

So what can be inferred from the differences in the responses to the pictures? It is clear that the immediate strategies that children have for interpreting such scenes are different. Children in the advantaged groups clearly brought into play strategies which, as it were, injected meaning into the situation. For example, they spontaneously looked for possible justifications for their judgements as, for instance, when speaking about the girl, Jane says 'She's looking worried because she doesn't know what's going to happen really'; or Colin says about the bus driver, 'He thinks he might knock the boy down because he thinks his brakes aren't very good'.

The advantaged groups were five times as likely to offer such spontaneous *justifications*, and were much more likely to give *justifications* in response to questions as, for example, David:

He didn't want to run the boy over because he didn't like it, because it's a very sad thing if you run somebody over.

There were signs of the development of mature conceptualisations amongst children in the advantaged group, for example, in response to the question 'What is the bus driver thinking?', Nigel uses a projective strategy:

How to stop, because he doesn't want to be responsible for the boy being run over.

In some instances there was evidence of awareness of conditions that might govern the outcome, for example:

John: If the bus driver hasn't seen the boy he might get knocked down

and of *possible alternative consequences*:

He might get hurt or killed.

Interpretations of the kind illustrated in these examples were three times more likely to be made by the children in the advantaged groups than by the children in the disadvantaged groups.

From this it would seem that the children have learned to interpret pictures on different bases, by the age of 5 and 7 years. This does not seem likely to be because children actually 'see' the picture differently. There were, for example, no differences found between the groups of children in the number of references which were made to objects and people in the pictures. All the major items were identified by all the children, but the implications of what was seen, and the inferences that could be made on the basis of what was seen, were much more frequently expressed by the children in the advantaged groups. The meanings that were expressed by the advantaged children were more complex, and depended more upon insight into possible relationships and causes than did the meanings expressed by the disadvantaged groups.

And yet it was shown that by a series of prompts and directive questions the disadvantaged children could be helped to recognise possible causes and relationships which had hitherto been neglected. In other words, much of the meaning that the advantaged child imposed spontaneously on the situation could be realised by the disadvantaged children if they were supported by questions and comments that 'led' them to such interpretations, as in the following example of 7-year-old Andrew:

J T: Will you tell me what you think is happening here?
         Tell me as much as you can about it, will you?
A: It's about a boy and that girl and there's a bus as well.
J T: Anything else?
A: Traffic lights.
J T: Mm . . .
A: And he's on the road.
J T: Anything else?
A: No . . . well that's post office isn't it?
J T: What do you think the bus driver's thinking?
A: He shouldn't do that.
J T: Why is he thinking that?
A: Cos he is.
J T: What do you think this person (waving) is thinking?
A: The same . . . 'He's silly'.

J T: Why does she think that?
A: He'll get knocked over.
J T: What will happen if the boy gets knocked over?
A: He'll have to go to hospital.
J T: Anything else?
A: She'll get into trouble.
J T: Why do you think that?
A: Cos she shouldn't have let him.
J T: Have you seen the traffic lights?
A: Yes . . . they say go.
J T: Why shouldn't the boy be on the road?
A: Because the lights are telling the bus to go.
J T: What will the driver try to do do you think?
A: He'll try to stop.
J T: Why will he try to stop?
A: Well he doesn't want to knock the boy down.
J T: Why not?
A: He could kill him couldn't he?
J T: Well what do you think the girl is trying to do?
A: She's trying to stop him from getting knocked down.
J T: Why does she do that?
A: Cos she thinks the bus is coming and it won't stop.

This seems to be a tortuous way, for both teacher and child, to express meaning that other children would give spontaneously in the immediate response. From this child's response it would seem that he has the resources with which to make an interpretation, but either he is not aware of his own knowledge and needs help to bring it into a structure that is acknowledged and expressed, or the meaning is at hand but he does not see the necessity for expressing it. He is, therefore, either unaware of the interpretation that he might make, or he does not feel that it is appropriate to express his interpretation. We cannot tell from this which is the more likely explanation. What can be seen is that the disadvantaged children, at 5 and at 7, tended to give short responses which indicated that the picture was interpreted, not as a whole, but object by object, and that there was a general failure to *infer* possible relationships, causes and consequences from the visible evidence. It seems then that the children were orientated to examine the situations differently and this was reflected in the more frequent use of different strategies of language.

Chapter 10

Beyond the Concrete Present

What explanations can be offered of the differences which emerged between the groups of children in the study in the kinds of interpretations they placed on the scenes depicted in the pictures shown to them?

Lying behind the kind of response the child will make is his capacity for benefiting from his experience. Even the young child comes to modify his behaviour on the basis of what has happened to him on previous similar occasions. But how can the child deal with his past experiences, organising them so that they can be accessible for dealing with new experiences? Since he cannot relive earlier experiences, he must somehow bring earlier experiences into present situations to act as some kind of measure or model. This is made possible only by finding some means of representing earlier experiences in ways that allow selection of the elements that are relevant to the new situation to be made.

A System for Representation

The model of 'instrumental conceptualisation' put forward by Bruner proposes some possible explanation of the ways in which 'memories can be organised in forms which can be drawn on readily' (Bruner, 1964). In Bruner's views, representation refers to those systems by which experience can be coded.

If we are to benefit from contact with recurrent regularities in the environment, we must represent them in some manner. To discuss this problem as 'mere memory' is to misunderstand it. For the most important thing about memory is not storage of past experience, but rather the retrieval of what is relevant in some usable form. This depends upon how past experience is coded and processed so that it may indeed be relevant and usable in the present when needed. The end product of such a system of coding and processing is what we may speak of as a representation. (Bruner, 1964, p. 2)

The first level of the organisation of memories referred to by Bruner seems to have much in common with Piaget's 'sensori-motor intelligence'. This mode of representation he describes as the 'enactive mode', and in this mode past events are represented through appropriate motor responses. Thus much of our general motor control in new situations requires little active reflection, but the knowledge to be drawn on for appropriate responses resides in the schemas of actions that can be brought into play. For example, riding a bicycle, changing gear when driving, mounting stairs, all may be performed smoothly as the required motor actions are released. Past experiences are drawn together as motor schemas and are ready and waiting to serve as required 'knowledge' for making present responses.

The second mode of representation Bruner refers to as the 'iconic mode' and in this form of representation events are summarised:

by the selective organisation of percepts and of images, by the spatial, temporal and qualitative structures of the perceptual field and their transformed images. Images 'stand for' perceptual events in the close but conventionally selective way that a picture stands for the object pictured. (Bruner, 1964, p. 2)

It is difficult to discover the part played by imagery in the young child's learning, but it would seem to give explanations for much of the child's intelligent dealings with his experiences long before language becomes a means for communicating with him. In his early play we see him often looking for objects that are needed but not in sight. Such intentional searching seems to suggest that he must be able to represent both objects and possible 'hiding places' to himself. In such behaviour it would seem that the child must be referring to images that are established by earlier experiences.

Finally, the third mode to develop is 'a symbol system that represents things by design features that include remoteness and arbitrariness' (p. 2). Through this mode experience can be represented by symbols and signs and the development of language can go ahead. But whereas the enactive and iconic modes of representation arise from within the individual, language is culturally determined and is taken within the individual from outside, and aids the organisation of experience, as well as serving as a means of communication. Language represents reality, so, argues Bruner, reality and language must in some way be organised similarly. It is not the case, he argues, that language is imposed upon experience but

Rather, language comes from the same root out of which symbolically organised experience grew. (Bruner, 1966, p. 44)

So it appears that we are innately programmed to construct our inner models of the world and our language in the same way. But language and organised symbolic experiences, that is, established images, only begin to relate to one another when the child is between 2 and 3 years old and language not only becomes part of experience but begins to modify it. Language is able to modify experience only because it springs from the same innate capacity of the organism to organise experience, and because meanings for experiences are shared in a social world.

To begin with, then, the child's organisation and representation of experience is in terms of action. 'Knowing' lies in familiar actions, and first words symbolise these actions. But then the child is also able to retain images of the world he experiences. These images aid the development of the child's thinking: the iconic mode of thinking provides a basis for words to symbolise the concrete picturable aspects of the world. Now language matches the experiences that are organised as images, and this extends to the child the possibilities of examining the world in its absence, as it were. He can now use past experience in the present, making it exist through the presence of symbols.

But as the child's model of language develops, it converges with the maturing organisation of experience, and the structure of language begins to exert an influence on the structuring of experience. Since the structure demanded by language is often more evident than the structure of experience, so language begins to exert an ordering effect upon experiences. Language can now not only refer to present and past experiences: in the symbolic mode language itself represents experiences, so that language can be treated as though it were experience itself, and it can be used to set up possible models of experience that do not exist in themselves in the present and past, but extend to projected experiences, possible future experiences, and allow the inspection of hypothetical situations.

Basic to Bruner's 'instrumental conceptualisation' model is the notion that our knowledge of the world is based on a model of reality that is both constructed and constrained by innate factors of the 'sensori-motor' system. The models of the world that the individual constructs result from the uses to which he puts the models, and these uses are essentially determined by the use his culture presents to him. There is great pressure in a technical society, Bruner claims, to bring action, image and language into a coherent relationship with one another. The inner model of the world that we build is then essentially and predominantly linguistic, that is, it is symbolic and abstract, and therefore a model that children can only gradually assume.

From the age of 4 onwards, Bruner sees language coming to play an increasingly powerful role as an implement of knowing, beginning to shape and augment the earlier enactive and iconic modes and, finally, superseding them. The translation of experience into the symbolic form of language allows the child to use remote reference, and the possibilities that are opened up for intellectual growth take the child far beyond anything that he can do with the image-forming system.

As the child learns to use language, then, he begins to be freed from operating only on the immediate situation, and operations on represented experiences become possible. So the child can not only represent to himself, and to others, elements of his past experiences, he can begin to represent to himself possibilities of experiences that lie beyond the present: he can project into the future, or consider happenings that are remote from him.

The 5-Year-Olds' Dealings with Past Experience

But we may ask whether this is an automatic process, that is, whether, with the development of language, experience necessarily is organised in such a way that the child can operate on situations in their absence. We have already seen in the study of the use of language by 3-year-olds that significant differences emerged between the advantaged and disadvantaged groups in the extent to which they spontaneously used language to refer to past experiences, or to look forward towards possible future experiences. The extent to which children in the disadvantaged groups were tied to the present ongoing concrete situation had been a distinguishing feature.

Children in the advantaged groups frequently returned to past experience without provocation other than that brought about by association with something the child or his companion had said. But, at the age of 5, further differences emerged in the responses the children made, in a situation that deliberately set out to examine the way in which they could recall and represent something of their past experiences.

There are problems in trying to examine the child's ability to recall past experiences. We considered asking the child to tell about some of his activities at home, or on holiday, but concluded that it would be difficult to ensure that we should necessarily select something of interest for each child.

It was decided therefore to use an experience that all children were likely to have met. After a trial run with a group of 5-year-olds it seemed that we could expect that all children would have been to a circus, or seen one on television, and therefore would know what a clown was and would be able to recall some incidents from their own experiences.

A novelty 'clown' which righted itself when knocked down was used. The children were first asked what they thought it was and they had no difficulty in identifying it as a clown. Then they were asked to tell about an occasion on which they had seen a clown and to relate something about the clown's activities at the time they saw him. Only three children, one from the advantaged and two from the disadvantaged groups, claimed that they had not seen a clown, although they were able to identify the doll as a clown.

The child was not hurried with the description. He found the doll attractive and as he talked about it, and explored its properties, the observer looked for an opportunity to have him recall and describe what he had seen a clown do. Once the child had been asked 'What did the clown do when you saw him?' the observer then supported the child's efforts with nods and the phrases 'Anything else?', 'Can you tell me anything else?'

Some of the children at first gave only general statements:

> He was right funny.
> He acted silly.
> They do daft things.

Then they referred to the actions of clowns and to the presence of animals and other people and their actions. They referred to objects, buckets or baths of water, steps, swings, 'he fell off a rope and got all soaked', 'one held the ladder and the other went up it'.

Some children identified with the feelings or characters of the people. Tom referred to one of the circus men as a 'serious man, who was scared and came down to see what was the matter – but he slipped and fell into the water. But he wasn't really drowned, thank goodness!'

Several of the children used comparisons or similes to make their descriptions:

Jill: We saw a clown at the circus. He had a long, long neck and his nose was like a beak. He had arms and legs like a clown but he had a hat on top of his head like – like a tramp. And he did all funny things – he had a brush and comb and he had a pair of scissors and he cut another clown's hair.

The last examples are taken from the responses of the children in the advantaged groups. Not all the answers were as full as these, but all the children referred to actions and situations and used terms that described the clown or his actions. Their responses suggested that they were conjuring up a picture of the incidents they remembered at the circus, almost as though they were reviewing the scene and giving a running commentary on what they saw.

Other children responded in strongly narrative style, for example:

Jonathan: Once I've seen a clown – I've been to Chipperfield's Circus. The clowns were very funny. Do you know what they did? One spilled paint over his hat and do you know what happened? He got up and fell down on the ground again because he had a pudding thrown in his face. And do you know he threw a pudding back at them. And then he threw cakes at the audience and at daddy and me. And he tore a hole in his trousers. He was wearing bright ones – and he sat down on a nail and then dragged the nail along, and his trousers fell off.

Jonathan was one of the few children who remembered visiting a real circus, and the rest either immediately stated that they had seen a clown on television, or after first saying that they hadn't seen a clown, handled the toy and talked about it and then recollected seeing a clown on television. Some of the children showed that they were aware that the clown they were referring to was not seen in the circus context proper. Janet, for example, explains:

Janet: Well I've seen one on television, but it's on the Circus Boy. He doesn't do his act on that – he doesn't do it. No it's more like a sort of programme where everything goes wrong. Something wrong always happens – like once it all went on fire, and one clown fell into a bath full of water. It's like when I went to see Harry Worth at the pantomime – and he was doing his face and one gets paste all over him and one was covered up all over his face with paste.

Catherine first declares that she cannot remember anything, but then goes on to give considerable detail about events.

Catherine: No ... I've not been to a real one ... I've seen one on television. You see it was under the big top. And er ... I can't remember but it was right funny I know. Well I *can* remember once that ... you see there was this clown climbing up those steps and he got on to his swing and he fell down off it. And he fell on top of an elephant and he sat upon its back. And this was on television in black and white.

Perhaps several of the children were doing more than just reporting on the scene they held as images that could be viewed 'inwardly' and matched through language. They showed that they were also projecting into the consequences of what was happening, showing an awareness of the possible discomfort of some of the stooges, who were 'soaked' or 'covered with paste' or 'lost their trousers'. Several also were commenting on the nature of the situation: it was all 'just pretend' or 'only an act', or 'it didn't hurt really' or 'it was made to look as though he was on fire'. These kinds of insights suggest that children are not interpreting the recalled scene at its face value but are taking into account the setting, and the role of 'clown' – an extension of meaning that is not easily drawn from the concrete display alone.

Such interpretations were not voiced by children in the disadvantaged groups. Their initial responses tended to be much shorter. The mean length of response to the request 'Tell me about the clown you saw, what did he do?' and the two supportive prompts, 'Anything else?', 'What else did he do?', was just over twenty words for the disadvantaged groups and fifty-four words for the advantaged groups.

The first response of the disadvantaged children was either to say they didn't know or to give a general statement with no reference to detail, for example:

> He acted silly.
> He did funny things.
> He makes you laugh.
> He was doing all sorts.
> He played it silly.
> He was just a joker.

Generally there was little spontaneous support or evidence given in these statements. They were, in fact, statements that could have referred to all clowns and little recognition was given to the specific acts by which such judgements could be made.

But it would be a mistake to infer from these initial responses that the disadvantaged children had actually seen less or remembered less about the scenes they had witnessed than the advantaged children. With persistence and encouragement and waiting for answers, it became clear that these children retained images of the actual scene and were able to refer to it.

For example, after Gwen had given a general judgement 'He was silly' and the routine follow-up question 'What did he do that was silly?' had brought the response 'He did silly things':

J T: Yes what silly things did he do?'
Gwen: Like clowns . . . that's what he did.
J T: But what were the clowns doing?
Gwen: Being silly.
J T: Anything else?
Gwen: No . . . they're always silly.
J T: What else can you tell me about the clown you saw?
Gwen: He did funny things.
J T: But what sort of things did he do that were funny?
Gwen: He muckied all his hair.
J T: However did he do that?
Gwen: Put water in and paint in and put his hat on.
J T: And then what happened?
Gwen: All paint went down him.
J T: Anything else?
Gwen: Then he put it on.
J T: Yes what else can you tell me?
Gwen: He had glasses on.
J T: He had glasses on . . . what did he do then?

Gwen: He went and put his glasses down and got paint on putting back his glasses.

J T: What else did he do?

Gwen: He fell downstairs.

Gwen represents those children in the disadvantaged groups who were able to tolerate the persistent questioning without which, it seemed, they were expecting to give very short answers. But it was not the case that the children in the disadvantaged groups talked less readily to the observer in other informal situations; rather it seemed that the children in the disadvantaged groups did not expect to give a 'full' interpretation, and assumed that they should meet questions with minimum responses.

When they were pressed further, it was clear that the children in the disadvantaged groups had a good deal more knowledge about clowns than they were inclined to communicate to the interviewer. It is difficult to decide what this reticence stemmed from, but the relationships between interviewer and individual child always appeared to be relaxed and all children volunteered information of a personal nature during the course of the interview, for example, 'I'm going swimming after school', 'My mum's taking me to the pictures tonight', 'We're going to my grandma's for tea', 'My dad's getting some pigeons tonight'.

All that can be inferred from this is that in this context, and others that were used, the children in the disadvantaged groups did not refer to past experience as explicitly and readily as did the advantaged groups. They tended to give shorter answers, and produced descriptions of fewer incidents spontaneously than did those in the advantaged group. On the other hand, with persistence from the interviewer, the children in the disadvantaged groups showed that they had observed and remembered the antics of the clowns they had seen.

When we recall past experience there is no doubt that we are dependent for the most part on language as the means of communicating our memories to others. Some reference, or some question in the present situation, leads us to inspect with 'an inward eye' recalled events or situations. Sometimes, perhaps, as we do this we are conscious that we are calling up images of those events and trying to inspect them almost as though they were scenes in the present so that we may report on them. Sometimes we are conscious that we cannot reproduce the scene inwardly and so say we just cannot remember. At other times, perhaps, we feel that we have clear images of the events or situation we want to communicate about but that matching them with verbal accounts is too difficult. Often we bring gesture, or role play to our aid, or draw a diagram, picture or map, or demonstrate through the use of other materials, or use similes and analogies to help us make our meaning clear. Often, too, we appeal to the other to use his own past experience of similar situations: 'You know what I'm talking about, don't you?'

But frequently, also, we are not aware that we are using visual or kinaesthetic imagery as a basis for recall. If images are there they are glimpsed momentarily; we are more conscious of the inner verbalisations that we use as we consider what we can say. Indeed, it seems that, as Bruner proposes, language has taken over from imagery, and there may be little vestige of gestures as evidence that the language we are using is supported by images built up from earlier experiences. At the age of 3 years the children from the disadvantaged group used language for recalling past experiences infrequently. Now again, at 5, we could see that although all children showed that they could refer to past experiences through the use of language, the children in the disadvantaged group used language for this purpose much less readily than children from the advantaged group, and gave much less information in their first responses.

But past experiences must form the basis from which we are able to set a structure upon the ongoing present experience, and we know that when we meet a situation that is in many ways 'new' or 'novel' we turn to those experiences that seem to have something in common with the present, as we search for an interpretation, or meaning, to guide our responses; moreover, past experience, and the interpretation of present experience, must provide the basis from which events in the future can be anticipated.

Projecting through the Imagination

Thinking about the future seems to be an exercise in projecting on the basis of past experiences and using the imagination, as it were, to get a glimpse of what the future situation might be like and to look at the possible alternatives that may operate in that situation. The ability to project into the possibilities of situations seems to be important, as the basis of all anticipation, prediction and hypothesis. At the age of 3 there had been evidence that thinking of this kind was only beginning to come within reach. When the children were 7, we devised a situation that allowed us to look at the way in which the child was disposed to project through the imagination and to think about possible alternative interpretations or explanations of some suggested event.

Three cards were prepared in which a matchstick figure was set against a background that might be interpreted in a number of different ways.

The first card showed a stick figure walking up an incline but there was no sketched-in detail, or suggestion of detail. The question asked was 'What might he see when he gets to the top?'

The second card showed a stick figure standing by a door that was slightly open. It was likely to be interpreted as someone entering or leaving a room or a building, or someone listening outside a slightly open door, or someone peeping into a room or building. The question was asked, 'What do you think he might see?'

The third card showed a stick figure in a position likely to be interpreted as 'running' and the few sketched lines in the background suggested a corner. The question put was: 'What might be happening here?'

Following the first response, two supportive prompts were given: 'Anything else?' or 'Why do you think he's . . .?' or 'What makes you think that?' Following that, a suggestion was made: 'What else might it be?' or 'What else might be happening?' This last question was put in order to see whether the child was aware of alternative interpretations.

The intention of this activity was to help the child show his ability to work through the imagination and build up a scene that would be compatible with the small amount of information given, and then to see what awareness the child had of possible alternative explanations.

The responses of the children to the picture outlines distinguished the advantaged groups from the disadvantaged groups. All the children in the advantaged group responded readily, although they tended to pause for some time before making first responses. All these children were able to develop a theme to some extent, although some responses were more elaborate than others. All the children were able to see at least one alternative to their first interpretation, and some saw it as a problem-solving situation in which they were motivated to find as many solutions as possible. The following are examples taken from the responses of children in the advantaged groups to the first picture, the stick figure walking up an incline. Angela's reply was typical of many:

Observer: What might he see when he gets to the top?
Angela: Well, he'll look down over the countryside and I think he will see farms, and farm houses and fields and animals cows and horses, perhaps . . . er . . . sheep in the fields.
Observer: Anything else?
Angela: Well there could be a road and some water . . . a river . . . couldn't there?
Observer: Anything else?
Angela: Well he might see hills . . . or mountains a long way off. Or he could see the sea . . . he might.

Many of the children in the advantaged group were very much aware that there was a size dimension in this imagined experience, for example Helen's response:

Observer: What might he see when he gets to the top?

Helen: Well, I expect he'd see the countryside all round him. Perhaps fields and woods . . . and he might see sheep and cows in the fields and there might be some farms . . . and they'd look small if they were a long way away.

Observer: Anything else?

Helen: Well . . . he could see a road perhaps going to a town . . . and then he'd see cars and lorries and things on the road. He might see buildings houses and shops and there might be a church and people . . . and they'd look very very small.

Observer: What else might he see?

Helen: Well he might see anything really . . . couldn't he? . . . hills and mountains . . . or he might see the sea . . . anything . . . you can't tell can you?

This last point was one made by only some of the advantaged group and not at all by any of the disadvantaged group. It seems to recognise that the solution is wide open. There is nothing in the picture to indicate what the figure might see – so the possibilities are numerous.

Some children like Jill are more specific about the detail of what might be seen:

Jill: He might see his friends which are very very titchy because he's so high up and um . . . he might see where he lived but it would be so tiny that he couldn't see it so well as a big block of flats.

Other children very quickly begin to place the figure in a story sequence, for example David:

David: It's a man I think, walking up a hill but I don't know why or where he's going.

Observer: What might he see from the top?

David: Well . . . he might be setting out on an adventure. He'll get to the top of the hill and he might see a castle down in the valley and perhaps houses and trees and a river.

Observer: Mm?

David: And they'll all look small because they're so far away. Perhaps he's looking for someone and he'll go down to the castle to find him.

And Helen gradually builds a setting for a story.

Observer: What might he see when he gets to the top?

Helen: He might see the world around him.

Observer: What might he see?
Helen: All people getting on buses and crowds . . . and tops of buildings and starlings running around. Oh . . . not running but I mean flying.
Observer: Anything else?
Helen: There'd be birds and at the other side . . . he can see the country.
Observer: What else might he see?
Helen: A few houses with lovely gardens and birds pecking at the seeds and field and farms . . . all sorts . . . animals and tractors.
Observer: Anything else?
Helen: He'd see a wood as well . . . a sort of shaded wood with all sorts of red benches in.
Observer: Anything else?
Helen: No . . . he ran into the wood and lived there. He built a hut cos he was lost and then he went up to the top of the hill to see where he could get to.

Not all responses from children in the advantaged groups were as long as these examples. Some answered quite shortly and were impatient to move on to the next card. Mark for example:

Observer: What might he see?
Mark: He'd be able to see whatever's on the other side . . . and he'll be able to see a very long way . . . especially if he's on Mount Everest.

The majority of children in the advantaged group described country or town scenes but each injected an element that was unique to them. One child talked about a shepherd, another about a bridge over a river, another about boats in the distance on the sea, another about mountaineers, another thought there might be a 'sheer drop' to rocks below. The majority of children readily extended the first idea or provided an alternative idea. We cannot tell from where their ideas came; it would seem likely that they could only spring from their own experiences, either direct experiences or by way of various experiences gained from films and television, or from stories and books and from what parents and teachers had told them.

By contrast children in the disadvantaged groups responded briefly, generally with a list of items that were not put into any overall setting. The following examples were typical and show dependence upon *labelling*:

1 *Observer*: What do you think he might see when he gets to the top?
   Lynne: A cottage.

Observer:	Yes ... anything else?
Lynne:	Snow.
Observer:	Yes snow ... what else might he see?
Lynne:	No ... nothing.

2	*Observer*:	What do you think he might see when he gets to the top?
	Pamela:	A big hole.
	Observer:	Yes ... anything else?
	Pamela:	(shakes her head)
	Observer:	What else might he see?
	Pamela:	I don't know.

3	*Observer*:	What do you think he might see when he gets to the top?
	Richard:	All sorts of things.
	Observer:	Yes ... what might he see?
	Richard:	Buildings.
	Observer:	Yes?
	Richard:	Cars buses lorries.
	Observer:	Anything else?
	Richard:	People ... shops ... some lights.
	Observer:	Anything else?
	Richard:	No.

4	*Observer*:	What do you think he might see when he gets to the top?
	David:	A slope.
	Observer:	Yes ... anything else?
	David:	No.
	Observer:	What else might he see?
	David:	Grass.
	Observer:	Anything else?
	David:	I don't know anything else.

Only four children from the disadvantaged group gave answers that were more extensive than the examples above, and these are given below. Elaine's was the longest response from all the children in the disadvantaged group.

Observer:	What do you think he might see when he gets to the top?
Elaine:	Water.
Observer:	Mm?
Elaine:	... and green . . and a green valley with big rocks up.
Observer:	Anything else?
Elaine:	And ... he might ... sea a little bird that's flying in the sky. And a little tiny bird in a nest up in the tree ...
Observer:	Yes.
Elaine:	And he might see tall big trees and big mountains behind it with acorns on. And he might eat them.

Observer:	Anything else?
Elaine:	He could sit down and eat all the acorns . . . and he was at another journey . . . and he would find an orange . . . and he would eat them all.
Observer:	What else might he see?
Elaine:	And then he would eat all the apples on the apple tree.
Observer:	Anything else?
Elaine:	No.

Nicholas, who lived on the top of a hill and could see the city beyond the fields immediately in front of his house, gave an answer which was different from any other.

Observer:	What do you think he might see when he gets to the top?
Nicholas:	He might see a nest. Or he might see a baby fox.
Observer:	Yes. Anything else?
Nicholas:	Or he might start climbing a tree if there is one at the top of it.
Observer:	Anything else?
Nicholas:	(shakes his head)
Observer:	What else might he see?
Nicholas:	Nothing else.

And Christopher, too, gave a unique response.

Observer:	What do you think he might see when he gets to the top?
Christopher:	Rocks grass and all the sky.
Observer:	Anything else?
Christopher:	And all the world.
Observer:	What else might he see?
Christopher:	A man coming. And the man might shoot him.
Observer:	Anything else?
Christopher:	He might shoot him cos there's some murderers about.

And Susan answers:

Observer:	What do you think he might see when he gets to the top?
Susan:	Might see a big hill going down.
Observer:	Yes . . . anything else?
Susan:	He would fall down if he's not careful.
Observer:	Yes anything else?
Susan:	Don't know.
Observer:	What else might he see?
Susan:	Don't know.

A number of examples have been quoted here to illustrate the problem of making an analysis and to demonstrate differences that are obvious to anyone reading the transcriptions. These differences are indicated when the mean number of words used in responses is calculated: for the disadvantaged groups the mean length of response is sixteen words and for the advantaged groups it is fifty-two words. Other linguistic measures also clearly differentiate the two groups. But these measures do not reflect the dramatic differences in the children's ability to 'think themselves into' the situation, an ability we have described as projection.

Could children's experiences of walking up hills have accounted for these differences? Were they just not familiar with looking down from the top of a hill? This hardly seems likely to be the case, since all the children were drawn from areas where steep slopes and views across the town or countryside were everyday occurrences. And for the most part the answers that were given indicated that the child knew the kind of elements that were likely to make up the scene, for example, houses, fields, cars were listed and offered as an answer. The difference lies in the structure into which the items are put. 'A valley, a village, a circus and caves' conveys very different meaning from 'There might be a valley with a goat eating grass. And plenty of other hills, and a village with a circus in it. And he might see some steps going down and caves with a lot of falling stones.'

We may not be justified in saying that for the children in the disadvantaged groups the picture outlines aroused very different uses of the imagination from those of the advantaged groups. But if this was not the case, then we must infer that they saw the necessity for expressing their imagining to the interviewer quite differently. Either the picture and the activity depicted in it had different meanings for the groups, or the situation in which they found themselves, being questioned by the interviewer had a very different meaning for them.

But perhaps we had chosen a subject for the picture that had not a great deal of relevance or interest for children in the disadvantaged group. Perhaps they would respond differently to the other pictures.

The picture of a stick figure peeping through a slightly open door received two different kinds of interpretation. The interpretations placed on this picture by the majority of children in the advantaged and disadvantaged groups were concerned with someone looking into a normal household and referred either to the contents or to the people inside the room or building.

A second interpretation used by a third of the children in both advantaged and disadvantaged groups was that the peeper saw something going on that was criminal, for example, he saw robbers, plotting or examining their loot.

The children in the advantaged groups once more tended to give more elaborate answers than the disadvantaged, for example David:

David: Well ... I think it's a policeman who's listening at the door and there's some robbers inside getting all the money and jewels.

He'll have to get some help with the policemen and he'll ask for a police car and some detectives to come and then they'll catch the robbers, you see.

And Angela gives a similar interpretation:

Angela: Oh dear ... I don't know ... let me see. Well ... I know ... there might be a gang of robbers in there and they might be plotting something ... like ... like robbing a bank or something.

Observer: Anything else?

Angela: And well ... the person, that person listening there ... well he would go and tell the police and they would rush up in cars and catch him.

Observer: Mm?

Angela: And ... well ... there might be a fight and someone could get hurt couldn't they?

Observer: What else might happen?

Angela: They'd get sent to prison I expect.

Several of the boys in the advantaged group saw the pictures as the illustration of a story, for example Andrew:

Andrew: Robbers! He could be a policeman and he could be listening to two robbers.

Observer: Anything else?

Andrew: Of course he'll get even in the end. He's going to Berlin ... just a minute ... could he be a spy in a police car and what would the driver say?

I expect there'll be some other policeman ... there'll be two at the front door and two at the back door.

Observer: Anything else?

Andrew: And perhaps there'll be an escape door. He'll be ... then they'll catch him.

The alternative interpretation of normal domestic activities is used by two-thirds of the children in both the advantaged and disadvantaged groups. Timothy's response is one of the more elaborate.

Timothy: He might be seeing his mum baking something that he likes and he can't have and so he might be licking his tongue. He might go in when his mum's gone upstairs and then he might sneak one and eat it in the cupboard or somewhere. And then his mum might come down and say 'Where's one of those cakes that I baked?' And um . . . then he might go outside and run away. And then his mother'll come searching for him and his mother would find him.

Some children showed awareness that there were many possible interpretations of the scene, for example Simon:

Simon: He might see some people you know and a table. And they might be sitting down playing a game and having a drink.
Observer: Anything else?
Simon: Well it might be a cobbler's shop and he is looking in. Seeing the cobblers making shoes.
Observer: Anything else?
Simon: It might be an ironmonger's . . . looking at all the hammers and the things and he might want to buy one.

In contrast, the interpretations given by the disadvantaged group tended to be shorter, and once more they tended to list the objects that might be seen as, for example, Richard does:

Richard: Some chairs.
Observer: Anything else?
Richard: Some carpets cupboards er er . . . chairs and er . . . television.
Observer: Anything else?
Richard: No.

David makes a similar response, before excusing his efforts.

David: Opening a door.
Observer: Anything else?
David: Furniture . . .
Observer: Yes, anything else?
David: No . . . I'm not a good thinker.

Nicholas gives a fuller interpretation:

Nicholas: He might see . . . his mum making some cakes and he wants one.
Observer: Anything else?
Nicholas: He might see a bottle of milk on the table and he wants that as well.

Julie lists the people:

Julie:	A lady.
Observer:	Anything else?
Julie:	A man.
Observer:	Anything else?
Julie:	A boy and a girl.
Observer:	Anything else?
Julie:	No.

Those children in the disadvantaged groups who gave the 'criminal-activity' interpretation also tended to respond with short phrases, for example:

David:	Robbers.
Observer:	Anything else?
David:	Getting money.
Observer:	Yes anything else?
David:	They've got a gun.
Observer:	Yes what else might be happening?
David:	He'll fetch police and they'll take them to prison.
Observer:	Anything else?
David:	No.

Only three children in the disadvantaged group gave more extensive responses which went beyond labelling and projected into possible activities. Elaine's was the longest of these:

Observer:	What might he see?
Elaine:	Two little children watching the telly and he might be not old enough to watch the television and er, he'd think that it was two little children going to come out of the door and he'd hide behind the wall and then he'd go back in because no one was there to bang on the door.

Here again we see the tendency for the responses of the advantaged groups to be longer and more complex interpretations than those offered by the majority of children in the disadvantaged group.

The third picture outline was designed so that there might be many possible interpretations and so that the child might be expected to see that there was a range of possibilities. The stick figure was unmistakably in a running position and the lines sketched in the background suggested a corner where the view round was obstructed by walls and buildings. There was nothing in the picture to suggest why the figure was running and the intention was to help the child to display his inclination to project through the imagination in order to put the figure into meaningful contexts and to see whether he appreciated the 'openness' of the situation for a range of equally possible solutions.

Interpretations of this kind must be made on the basis of past experiences whether they are real life experiences of the individual or vicarious experiences taken from accounts given by other people, or seen on television or gleaned from stories and books.

The children were asked 'What might be happening here?' All the children assumed that the figure was running and the first response was in terms of 'running away' or 'running to'. Several children, however, answered 'He's running' and this was then followed by the question 'Why do you think he's running?'

An answer that had not been expected, but one that was given by several children in the disadvantaged groups, was in terms of the reason for this judgement that the figure was running: 'Because I can see he is', or 'Because his legs are bent', or 'Because he's like this' as the child demonstrated a running position.

In answer to the question 'Why do you think he is running?' these 'literal' interpretations, if unexpected, are quite appropriate and are a logical response. But it is interesting that no child from the advantaged groups gave this kind of answer and all gave answers of a kind expected by the questioner. The difference in response here is interesting and could be judged as differences in the meaning of the question for the children. We shall return to a discussion of this and related issues in a later chapter. In these instances, the question was put again: 'Yes, but *why* might he be running?' and so the child was helped to look for a response of another kind.

What kind of experiences would children turn to in an effort to put the running figure into appropriate contexts? A third of the children in both groups met the question by suggesting contexts that seemed to relate to everyday experiences; for example, an explanation given by several children was to do with shopping.

Monica: Cos he might be in a hurry to go to the shop and it might be just closing, and he has to get his mam something.
Michelle: He might want to get to the shop there and it might be closing soon so he wants to get there right quick.

Other 'domestic' contexts referred to catching buses, or going to school or posting letters, for example:

Christopher: Because he's trying to catch a bus or he's going to meet someone or he's running to school because he's late.

Other interpretations within the 'domestic' context were based on children being 'in trouble' at home, or trying to escape from punishment by their parents, for example:

Alan: He's running away 'cos his mother smacked him.
Observer: Anything else?
Alan: He was naughty . . . he'd broken a cup.
Observer: Why else might he be running?
Alan: Because his mother's after him and she'll smack him and send him to bed.

Or the runner may be seen as running away from other people, as for example:

Mark: Someone's chasing him 'cos he's done something wrong.
Observer: Why else might he be running?
Mark: Because he's been chucking stones at people and they're after him.

Frequently the wrong doing was seen as leading to police action, as for example:

Robert: He might have done something wrong and somebody's chasing him.
Observer: Why else might he be running?
Robert: 'Cos if the police catch him they'll take him to prison.

The responses of eight children from the disadvantaged groups were based entirely upon the 'naughty–punishment' theme and included misdemeanours such as breaking windows, throwing stones, calling names or abuse, and the running figure was trying to escape from pursuers. The responses of the children from the advantaged groups included such incidents in their list of possibilities.

Six children from the advantaged groups and seven from the disadvantaged groups based their responses entirely or partly on 'criminal acts', for example:

Angela: Well he looks as though he is running away from somebody. Perhaps there is someone chasing him.
  He might have stolen something from a shop say . . . and the shopkeeper might be running after him or he might have got the police and they might be after him.
Observer: Why else might he be running?
Angela: He might be running to his house or his car . . . his car I think so he can get away from the police.

Several responses from children from both advantaged and disadvantaged groups made a 'robber' or 'thief' interpretation:

Garry: It's a robber running away and the police are after him. He bashed a window and pinched something . . . some jewels and some watches . . . and he's looking for somewhere to hide.

A third of the children from the advantaged groups met the question as though they had been asked to tell a story to explain the running figure, but no child from the disadvantaged groups interpreted the question in this way.

Timothy, for example, did not want the observer to make any comments but, assured of his audience, it would seem, enjoyed making up his story as follows:

Timothy: Perhaps he might . . . someone might have been knocked down by a car and he's running to tell his (the person knocked down?) mother to ring for an ambulance and the police and a fire engine.

    And then his mother would come and she might put her coat round him and she might go to the hospital with them. Then that boy might go and see him after and he might take him some sweets and some flowers.

    Then he (the person knocked down) would come out of hospital and he'll be able to run around again and then he might have some stitches that he'd got to have out. And then his friend might take him with him in his dad's car. And his dad's car might have a flat tyre.

Other stories were based on 'criminal' themes, for example:

Alan: This man was a robber. He'd just robbed a jewellery shop and now he's running away to where the getaway car was. And the police were chasing him.

    He had to run very, very fast. He was such a fast, so fast, such a fast runner that he smashed a . . . he got in through the back window . . . and he smashed it. And then the getaway car started driving and he was in, safely in the car. You see, he got away ready to do the next robbery.

The differences in the responses given by children to the same question are to the reader of the scripts quite dramatic and clearly may be due to a number of different factors that need to be examined. But the differences so far referred to have been differences in the contexts 'invented' for the running man. Other differences emerged that must also be considered when we begin to look at the differences in meaning that the whole interview situation seemed to have for the children involved.

One aspect of this particular part of the investigation was to try to examine whether the child at 7 appreciated the 'openness' of the task and the range of possible meanings that could be imposed on the 'running figure'. This was an aspect of the children's responses that clearly differentiated the advantaged and the disadvantaged groups. It is difficult to measure some of the differences in the 'quality' of responses that have been illustrated by the above examples, but it is not difficult to recognise the alternative possibilities. Some children immediately saw the implications of the openness of the question and after a pause produced several alternatives in the first utterance, as for example:

Sally: He might be running to catch a bus, or train . . . or he might be running to catch his friend . . . or his mother . . . or he might be running to a shop that's just about to be closed.

Although some children kept their original theme of 'everyday activities' throughout, others saw that there were not only 'running to' and 'running from' explanations but also 'everyday' and 'criminal' explanations, for example:

Simon: He might be late for school or for his music lesson. Or he might be running to the bank before it closes, or running to the shops before they close, because if he wasn't running they might close before he gets there.

Or it might be a thief who's stolen something and the police might be after him or he's running to get away quick before they find out.

No child in the disadvantaged groups gave more than one alternative in response to the question, but seven gave an alternative in answer to the follow-up questions, for example:

Observer: What might be happening here?
Linda: He's running.
Observer: Why do you think he's running?
Linda: Because I can see he's running fast.
Observer: Why might he be running?
Linda: To get a bus . . . because he will be late for work.
Observer: Anything else?
Linda: No.
Observer: Why else might he be running?
Linda: He could be a robber and a policeman is running after him.

The child from the disadvantaged groups who gave the four alternatives with some help was David, who had earlier excused himself by saying he was 'not a good thinker', but he reached four only after several additional questions from the observer, as follows:

Observer: Why do you think he's running?
David: He could be playing races.
Observer: Yes . . . anything else?
David: No.
Observer: Why else might he be running?
David: I don't know.
Observer: I'm sure you do. Why else might he run away?
David: He could be a robber running away from a policeman.
Observer: Anything else?
David: No that's it.
Observer: But couldn't he be running away from something else?
David: Someone could be chasing him.
Observer: Anything else?
David: He could be running to fetch some bread or something.
Observer: Anything else?
David: No that's all.

Other children in the disadvantaged groups also showed that with persistent questioning and support they could produce a number of different alternatives.

We have quoted a good deal from the recorded conversations in order to make points about the abilities of children, at 5 and 7 years of age, to think and express their thinking through language, about situations that depend little on the ongoing concrete present experience.

We have perhaps little knowledge or evidence about the way in which thinking of the kind we have referred to as 'projection' can take place, or how it develops. It would seem to demand from the child that he marshal, as it were, his past experiences, and then use the elements of information that are available and try them for 'fit' against held knowledge and past experiences. 'Held knowledge' we would see as those concepts that have been built from a multiplicity of experiences and the abstraction of attributes and relationships that can be 'known' without the need for constant reference to memories of similar events.

The mental activity required in dealing with this last task, for example, is one of selecting for examination all 'running away' situations that have previously been met. It is hardly likely to be the case that children in the disadvantaged groups have had less experience of 'running away' situations in the context of everyday experience, or for that matter that they will have heard or seen less about 'robbers' and 'thieves' or 'racing' and the several topics that came up in the contexts put forward. In fact, taking the range of topics brought forward by the two groups, there is little difference. The domestic mishaps mentioned were very similar: everyday situations, catching buses, going to the post, going shopping, were all referred to by someone from each of the groups. So were 'naughty' activities outside the home: bullying, breaking windows, knocking on doors, 'pinching' something, all were used by someone from each of the groups.

The differences came in the amount of detail that was given and the number of alternatives supplied. The fact that the children in the advantaged groups said on average three times as much as those from the disadvantaged groups reflects not only the greater lack of completeness in the structure of the utterances produced, but also in the complexity of the utterances and in the detail given and in the complexity of the ideas produced.

The difference between the mean number of words used in responding to the projection pictures is also a reflection of the number of alternative interpretations offered. In the advantaged groups two children gave five alternatives and four gave four alternatives, with an average of three alternatives for each child. In comparison, three children in the disadvantaged groups gave three alternatives and four gave two alternatives; the remaining seventeen gave no alternatives and the average is for each child 1·5 alternative interpretations.

The facility with which children are able to deal with situations that ask them to operate away from the ongoing present seems, then, to differentiate the groups quite clearly. In referring to past experiences the disadvantaged group seem to be less aware of detail and to be less inclined to place their memories in a structure when they talk to others about them. When asked to project into possible explanations of situations, they appear to be less inclined to be explicit about their ideas and to be less aware of the possibilities that are open for making interpretations of the information given.

What implications might such differences have for the education of young children? We will leave this question for discussion in a later chapter.

Chapter 11

Language and Logical Thinking

In studying the way in which meaning develops for the young child, we cannot neglect some examination of the way in which he comes to understand the everyday phenomena by which he is surrounded. So far our discussion, and the examples given, have looked at the child's developing ability to interpret, or set a structure upon, the situation and events that he meets. We have looked at the way in which he organises the elements of experience in order to achieve an overall, or central, meaning, or to discover a range of possible alternative interpretations from which he might select the meaning to be imposed.

We are not at this stage arguing that the child's ability to use language as a means of expressing the structure that he is imposing is responsible for the structure that is imposed. All we would argue is that it is difficult for the listener to know that structure exists for the child, if the child is not able to express it. Moreover, we have seen that children in the disadvantaged groups frequently demonstrated that they 'knew' more than they were able, or willing, to express through language, except with considerable persistence on the part of the interviewer in questioning and supporting their efforts.

Where reasoning and explanation are needed as an indication to the adult (particularly to one who is acting in a tutorial role) of the child's understanding, the child must be at some disadvantage if he is unable to express his understanding of concepts that he has already established. Is it possible, then, that the handicap of many disadvantaged children stems more from their problems in communication than from their basic conceptual development?

This question raises issues that have interested psychologists and students of child development for many years and perhaps the arguments that have been sustained over that period have come to affect the way in which we regard the child's ability to learn in the early years.

Piaget's position is well known, and indeed he has brought forward powerful evidence to show that intellectual development proceeds as a result of the child's own actions upon objects, and the changes that come about in the underlying structure that develops through the process of what he refers to as 'equilibration'. The 'underlying structure' we could refer to as the 'meaning' that he is able to set upon particular experiences. Equilibration is effected by a dual process, referred to as *assimilation* and *accommodation*, which is the process by which new knowledge and new understanding are brought about, and refers in the first case to changing elements of experience so that they may be incorporated in the internal systems (that is the intellective processes) and in the second case to the modification made to the internal structure as a result of this assimilation (Piaget, 1952). The underlying structures, or schemas, so built up, continue to be modified as the assimilation–accommodation processes act upon experiences. Equilibration is achieved when the processes of assimilation and accommodation are in balance and successive periods of equilbrium give rise to recognisable stages of development.

Thus during the first two years, during which sensori-motor intelligence characterises the means by which the child comes to impose structure on his experiences, the schemas are built up by the direct intake of information through the senses and through motor action.

During the following stage, the *preconceptual phase* in Piaget's terms, the development of symbolism is paramount and because objects and actions can now represent whole sequences of events the child begins to use the developing schemas for modifying his behaviour, both with respect to past experiences and for the anticipation of pending experiences. With the establishment of language the child can now represent to himself and to others what he reveals through his own actions, and then 'his discoveries ... become *knowledge* of objects and events rather than *reactions* to objects and events'.

As the child moves into the conceptual stage of development, that is into the *concrete operational* stage, he still has problems of structuring his perceptions, he still is *reacting* to objects and events on the basis of his perceptions and the process of accommodation–assimilation has not yet enabled him to reconcile the several dimensions of his experiencing. Piaget's work on the concepts of number and spatial relationships illustrates very clearly the problems that children have in the years between 4 and 8. The child must *assimilate* the conflicting information that comes from his perception of the situation and *accommodate* it to form a structure in which the relationship between the changing elements of experiences is held firm and maintained, as he responds to many experiences that differ greatly in the direct ongoing information that is received, but embody the same relationship. We say that the child now has a particular concept, part of a system of schemas that operate to structure his experiencing, mediating the 'meaning' of his experiencing to him.

For Piaget, language serves to 'carry' the concept and represent ideas. 'The function of the concept (relation, class, etc.) ... is to interpret and comprehend, and its tendency from the start is towards legality and causal explanation and towards deductive reasoning. ... Words, then, merely designate conceptual articulations ...' (Piaget and Inhelder, 1966, pp. 382–3).

It is not, it would seem, that Piaget attaches little importance to language – 'the importance of language is a commonplace' (Inhelder and Piaget,

1964, p. 4) he states, almost as though its importance is so great and obvious that it needs no examination. Much of this work, however, neglects to consider the importance of the ongoing experience of language that accompanies much of the child's experiencing. It is one thing to argue that 'giving' the child the necessary language to deal with a concept does not enhance the development of the concept, but quite another to argue that the experiences of language in use make no impression on the child's inclination to respond to his experiencing. Although Piaget sees language as neither a sufficient nor a necessary condition for the development of concrete operational thinking, he seems to regard it as a necessary condition for logical thinking.

It is necessary because within the system of symbolic expression which constitutes language the operations would remain at the stage of successive actions without ever being integrated into simultaneous systems or simultaneously encompassing a set of interdependent transformations. Without language the operations would remain personal and would consequently not be regulated by interpersonal exchange and co-operation. It is in this dual sense of symbolic condensation and social regulation that language is indispensable to the elaborating of thought. (Piaget, 1954, p. 98)

In examining the way in which children in the study used language, we were concerned to discover whether any differences were developing between the groups in the ability to use language for logical thinking. We tried therefore to devise situations that would require explanations to be given and in which children would be motivated to give explanations if they could. We wanted to see the kind of strategies of thinking that the children would use to examine the problem and the way in which they would use language to meet the demands of the situation.

What are bridges for? This was a question that sprang from our journeyings to meet the children at their homes and at school when they were 3 years old. We had noted how frequently we found ourselves being directed to take bridges over rivers, canals, railways and roads. Living in Yorkshire towns and cities, it hardly seemed likely that 5-year-olds would not be familiar with the notion of a bridge. But what is a bridge for? Posing this question is asking the child to display not just his recognition of what is labelled as a bridge, but to display his basic understanding of the meaning of 'bridge'. This, then, was the idea that we decided to investigate with the children when they were 5 years old.

When the children were 7 years old we wondered to what extent they would be able to deal with explanations of familiar phenomena. The general practice of providing empty soft plastic bottles for water play in all the nursery and infants' schools suggested to us that all children would be familiar with the use of such bottles as 'squirters'. It seemed, therefore, that this phenomenon would perhaps offer a suitable situation in which to examine the child's ability to follow explanations and the strategies he would then employ in order to explain to others why such bottles made good squirters.

The Bridge Problem

Since we thought that 5-year-olds might not readily talk about bridges in the abstract, we set the problem in an activity context. A 'river' in blue plasticine was set upon a board, and a block of brown plasticine together with some thin strips of wood and an assortment of small cars and plastic boats, which might be used with it, were put together in a box. All the boats had sails or masts that made them deceptively tall.

The activity was used at the end of one session with the children so that there was no period of waiting to establish a relationship; it followed quite easily from the previous activity.

The problem was established: the blue plasticine was supposed to be a river, and people wanted to get across, a car was put on the board, and the point was made that the people in the car wanted to get across the river. What was the best way to do this? If the children did not reach the bridge solution after several efforts, in which their own suggestions had been accepted, they were told that a bridge was the usual solution and they were then asked to use the materials in the box to make the best bridge they could.

When they had finished they were asked if they thought their bridge was a 'good' one, and whether they thought it was or was not they were asked to justify their judgement. Then the small boats were taken out and placed on the river and they were asked what their judgement was now, and asked again to justify it. Then, if the bridge was too low, as it invariably was, they were asked to say how they would improve the bridge. When finally the boat could pass under the bridge they were asked why it was now a 'better' bridge, and finally they were once more asked the question 'Why do we need bridges?'

It can be seen that the task had a certain 'openness' about it that made it difficult for the interviewer to use identical strategies with all the children. The introductory statement and initial and final questions were the same in all the interviews, but the interviewer responded spontaneously to the child as the child made his bridge. All the children were interested to pursue the activity and talked quite readily about it, but there were differences, not only in the amount of talk, but also in the kind of strategies that children used in order to solve the problem.

Classification of Responses

The first question asked the children to think of the most satisfactory way to get cars and buses from one side of a river to the other. Although some children recognised the problem almost immediately, and other children did so after their first response had been echoed back to them, and they had thought again, more than half the children needed several more attempts before they reached the bridge solution spontaneously. This ready recognition of the 'expected' solution distinguished the advantaged and disadvantaged groups. Fourteen of the advantaged group spontaneously recognised 'bridge' as the solution, a further eight gave a further alternative before reaching the bridge solution and two children were given the solution after two or three further attempts.

In the disadvantaged group no child anticipated the bridge solution at the first attempt and only four at the second attempt. The remaining twenty needed between them eighty-nine attempts and in the end eighteen children had to be given the solution of 'bridge'. The solutions offered by the two groups are interesting.

In the advantaged group some children offered 'boat' as their immediate response and where the second response was not 'a bridge' the majority offered 'ferry boat'. Helen suggested 'tunnel' but on being asked what went through the tunnel she answered 'water' and it seemed that she was suggesting a 'road over a tunnel', and not 'a tunnel under a river' that would have been an apt solution also.

Other solutions offered by the advantaged group were:

David: Drive the cars through the water.
Andrew: They'd have to drive round the river or have an amphibious car to drive along.
Catherine: Paddle over if the water was shallow or row across.
Karen: Across a board – we've been across one at Appton Bridge.
Fiona: Stepping-stones you could go across.

Other alternatives put forward by children in the disadvantaged group included:

Michele: Well if the river wasn't there they could easy get across.
  If they buy a boat they could get easy across.
Austin: They'd have to do it by a crane. Or swim.
Pamela: Go on to a boat and swim over.
  Go round.
  Leave their cars and go over.
  Stride over it.
Joseph: Get a pole and jump over it.
  Go round the corner.

Susan: If they're little, well, they can't go across
             because they're tiny and they've to see the
             mothers if they can.
Elaine: If it's a water car it's all right.
             If it is not a water car, well you can't.

The problem for the 5-year-old, then, in the first place is one of con-
ceptualising the problem. To answer the question there has to be a realisation that there is an acknowledged way of dealing with the problem in
principle. It is a recognition that the question is not concerned with a
particular instance but is rather dealing with a definition.

Once the bridge solution had been established the children were then
encouraged to build a bridge with the plasticine, and then the plastic
boats were placed on the river and the child was asked to judge whether his
bridge was a 'good' bridge.

Generally answers could be made on the basis of the width of the bridge
(for the cars), the strength of the bridge (it must not fall down) and the
height of the bridge (the boat must pass under).

The children's responses sprang from three different bases. First, the
recognition of the problem and explanation of the solution, for example:

The boats can't go under so I'll have to make it higher.
It's going to fall down – I'll make the sides stronger.
It's all right 'cos the boats can go under.

Such responses use strategies of *reasoning* and are classified as *explanatory*.

A second basis was a recognition of the problem, but with a 'non-
solution' suggested, for example:

The boats can't go under so they'll have to knock the bridge down.
The boats can't go under so the people will have to get out and walk
around.

Responses of this second kind are in a reasoning mode but since a
solution is or not recognised or is inappropriate it is referred to as
pre-emptive.

The third type of response we refer to as *syncretic*, since the basis of the
judgement appears to be made on aspects that appear to bear no relationship to the problem set or to its solution, for example:

Why is it a 'good' bridge?
Because it looks nice.
Because they can sit on it.
Because no one will fall in.
Because I like making it.

Finally, the question is put, 'Why do we have bridges', and a follow-up question, depending on the first answer, 'And what about the boats', or 'What about the cars?' Again answers fell into three basic categories:

EXPLANATORY AND RELEVANT

The first type of answer *recognises causal and dependent relationships,* for example:

> So all these cars and people can get over the river and the boats have to go under it.
> The people can walk along it and the cars can drive over.

And what about the boats?

> It has to be high to let them go through.
> Traffic has to go over but boats must be able to get under.

PRE-EMPTIVE EXPLANATIONS

A second group are explanatory but are either not logical or not relevant. They are described as pre-emptive.

> Bridges are for boats to sail under them.
> Bridges are strong so they won't fall down.
> Bridges are so that people don't go in the water.

SYNCRETIC RESPONSES

And finally there are syncretic responses, the most frequent of which was 'Bridges are for boats'.

Judgements in the syncretic category are made on the basis of contiguity or of dominant attributes or personal feelings, but they are not explanatory, nor are justifications offered for the statements.

In this particular problem, placing the boats next to the bridge that the child has built gives a dominance to the relationship between the boat and the bridge. The boat clearly has to go under, although several children in the disadvantaged groups did not succeed in recognising this as a necessary condition. If the bridge is seen as an obstacle, solutions are offered like 'getting out and walking round', or 'the boat turns round and goes the other way'. But children must keep a firm hold on the idea that the bridge is to solve problems of getting over the water, and the height of the bridge is related to the secondary problem of not impeding boats.

The strategies that children used to meet this problem again differentiated the two groups. The disadvantaged group used more than twice as many syncretic and pre-emptive strategies as the advantaged group (seventy-three to thirty-one) and the advantaged group used more than three times as many relevant explanatory strategies as the disadvantaged group. There was some difference in the number of children in each group who ended by insisting that 'bridges were for boats'. There were eleven children in the disadvantaged group, and three children in the advantaged group who had not attained a stable concept of a bridge.

From these results it would seem that some of the disadvantaged children at least must have established the concept of a bridge in spite of the fact that they offered little in the way of logical explanations. On the other hand, it is true that they were much less able to support the judgements they made with logical explanations, and the orientation towards syncretic and pre-emptive responses would seem to indicate a lack of awareness of the reasons that can be given as justification for the statement that bridges are built in order to take people or traffic of some kind over obstacles.

To be able to make a statement to the effect that bridges are to take traffic over, and yet at the same time to be making judgements about a bridge that justify it being a 'good' or 'effective' bridge or not, by statements like 'I like it', or 'Bridges are made of stone' or 'The boats will knock it down', perhaps indicates that the concept is held at a level of intuition rather than at a level of awareness of the logical requirements of a bridge.

Thus we might consider that the outcome of this small investigation endorses the position taken by Piaget that the concept itself may exist without necessary support from language, but we can also see that those children who can justify and explain the basis of the concept they hold, that is, define it to themselves as well as to others, may be in an advantageous position in school where understanding tends to be measured in terms of the explanations that can be given.

Understanding 'How' and 'Why'

As children grow older, more and more of the situations they meet in school demand understanding of relationships; and frequently explanations, together with demonstrations of common phenomena, are offered by the teacher. How realistic are our expectations that by the age of 7 most children will be able to understand explanations and be able to give them in return to others?

When the children were 3 we had seen that many of the advantaged 3-year-olds spontaneously offered explanations to each other and to the adult; they were not always appropriate or logical explanations, it is true, but it seemed that they were developing an orientation towards looking for causal relationships, and giving explanations of processes. At that age there was little from the children from the disadvantaged groups that suggested any inclination towards offering explanations readily.

When the children reached $5\frac{1}{2}$ we have seen that the children from the disadvantaged groups gave appropriate explanations less readily than the advantaged children, and even where the concept was apparently held they still were inclined to make judgements on a syncretic basis and not to look for causal relationships.

In order to investigate the way in which the use of language for logical thinking was developing, we wanted to see how the children would attempt to explain why plastic bottles make good squirters. All children know that this is so: there was no doubt that they could all pick the bottle up, put it in the water, squeeze it and fill it, or partly fill it, and then squirt the water out again. So the task we were setting them dealt with a very familiar activity. They all knew the sequence of actions in an operational sense; but would they be able to explain the sequence to someone else and could they understand the conditions, or principles by which it worked, if they were explained to them?

The child was introduced to the problem by an invitation to use a plastic bottle as a squirter. Then the interviewer asked the child why the bottle made a good squirter, and through questions and comments the following points were demonstrated and explained simply.

1 That it was only because the bottle was flexible and could be squeezed, and would return to its original shape when released, that it could be a squirter.
2 That when the air had been expelled by squeezing and the nozzle was placed below the surface, the water was drawn in as the bottle returned to its original shape.
3 That water could only be squirted out because the sides of the bottle were flexible and collapsed when squeezed.
4 That when water was forced through a narrow hole in a short tube, or the nozzle (this term was not used), it formed a jet.

All the children began by making a running commentary on their actions and at each point the interviewer intervened to ask why it should be so and offer explanations. When the whole sequence had been discussed the child went to bring a friend in and was asked to explain to his friend why a plastic bottle made a good squirter. All the children used the plastic bottle to demonstrate and explain the process.

It is not easy to find a basis for comparison. There was a difference once more on the mean number of words used to give an explanation; the advantaged groups had a mean of fifty words, whilst the disadvantaged groups had a mean of thirty-five words, but length alone is not necessarily an indication of superiority in the explanations offered. There were examples of long rambling comments that explained little. On the other hand it was impossible to explain with a short answer.

Generally the answers which gave all or most of the points tended to be long, but there were two concise answers which included the main points, for example:

Tom: It's because when you squeeze it, it's not hard, and so all the air is pushed out. Then when you put it in the water and don't squeeze, the sides go back and so the water goes in and takes the place of air. Then you squeeze and the water is forced through the little hole up the tube and makes a jet.

This answer was judged to have given the essential four points.

Most children commented as they demonstrated the use of the plastic bottle, but six from the advantaged groups and two from the disadvantaged groups took up the role of demonstrator, as in the examples below:

Alan: Look Stephen . . . it is a good squirter . . . watch.
Stephen: Yes I know . . . I do that sometimes.
Alan: Well watch . . . I'm squeezing the sides 'cos they're soft . . . and all the air has to come out . . . feel. (Alan demonstrated in Stephen's face)
Stephen: Yes . . . I can feel it blowing.
Alan: So it's all out . . . right . . . now put the hole under the water like that. Now . . . let go . . . and the sides are straightening out . . . so the water has to come in to fill it up . . . where the air was. Now . . . take it out and squeeze the sides . . . and it pushes the water through that little hole and it comes out . . . like a water pistol, isn't it?

Gary's response was the fullest of the answers from the disadvantaged group.

Gary: Watch Peter.
You've got to squeeze the bottle like this.
A glass one doesn't squeeze.
Then you put it in water and it comes in . . . well it should.
(he has a little difficulty with the bottle)
There it's filled up now . . . and a bit of air's come in as well.
Now watch.
I'm squeezing it hard.
Then it squirts out . . . 'cos I'm squeezing it out . . . I'm squeezing it out and the air's pushing it out.

Although many children referred to the little hole, few explained the jet feature fully. Janet tries to explain this:

Janet: It came out in a long jet . . . because of the lid . . . this part shaped like a long thin shape.
And it . . . and you . . . and
if you squeeze it it only allows water to go out a bit at a time . . . in a long jet.

Many children, although offering what were meant to be full explanations, showed that they had problems of understanding. For example, they reversed the relationship and saw the air pushing the water out, instead of water replacing the air that has been pushed out. Deborah used the word pressure, which had not been used in the discussion with the interviewer.

Deborah: When you've squeezed it in the water there's pressure in. But when you let go pressure is going out . . . no . . . coming in. Well . . . when the bottle's in the water there's no pressure but when you stop squeezing it the pressure's coming in and its bringing the water in with it.
Then you squeeze again and it squirts because the pressure is forcing the water out.

Although twenty from the advantaged groups expressed at least two of the basic principles stated above, the remaining four gave quite long answers but showed that they had considerable difficulty in understanding the causal relationship between the attributes of the bottle and the subsequent jet. Mandy gave an answer that was very much in a reasoning 'mode' but that failed to establish any of the relationships save that between the final 'squeezing' and the consequent jet.

Mandy: This is how I think it does it.
It's the air drawing the water up into the bottle.
The air's going out and the water's coming it.
Then you squeeze it and the water's separating and so there's a space where you'd squeezed it . . . and you squash it again and the water shoots out because its a little hole through there.

We can see from answers like this that although the child's resources of language may be good, the thinking expressed may be quite confused. Nevertheless it would seem that Mandy has an expectation about the kind of exploration that is appropriate and this at least is expressed in her talk. Her talk also demonstrates to her listener the extent of her problem of understanding and might lead to further demonstrations and explanations in order to help her get it right. Expressing thinking in language so that others may inspect it is one way of demonstrating to others the help that is needed.

Many of the children in the disadvantaged group, however, demonstrated a very different characteristic: they tended to so reduce their explanations that it was impossible for the listener to judge how much they understood. For example, Michele:

Michele: You get this and you put it in here like this.
And then you squeeze it. And then some bubbles come and you put your side in.
And then you get it out and squeeze all the water out like that.

As Michele talks she is demonstrating and it is clear that she knows the sequence of the action. She may here be indicating her understanding of the characteristic of the bottle – 'you put your side in and then you get it out'. But it is very difficult for the listener to judge from her talk how much she understands.

Linda is another example of a child who may understand a great deal but who fails to make clear what she understands.

Linda: Put that into there.
Water goes through there into the bottle.
And it goes flat when I press it down.
Bring it out.
Make it round again.
Put it back in.
Let some more water go in.
Make it round again.
Aim it at the water and squeeze it back in.

But many more of the disadvantaged groups gave answers that matched their actions and expressed little as explanation, for example Mark:

Mark: You get it like that.
You squeeze it.
Go like that.
And go like that.

And yet Mark was able to recognise the relationship between the attributes of the bottle and its squirting properties as the observer pursued the topic by further questioning.

Observer: Why does this bottle make a good squirter?
Mark: Cos it's like that. (he demonstrates squeezing)
Observer: Yes . . . but what does 'like that' mean?
Mark: You squash it . . . with your hand.
Observer: Well . . . what does that do?
Mark: Pushes it out.
Observer: Pushes what out?
Mark: Pushes the air out . . . and it pushes the water out.
Observer: Why does the water get into the bottle?
Mark: Cos the air's gone out.
Observer: Anything else?
Mark: Cos it goes . . . round again. (the bottle returning to its original shape, presumably)

We are left with the question that has come up time and time again. Do the children in the disadvantaged groups 'know' less about the world around them than the advantaged group? Or do they for some reason 'express' less about what they 'know'? Or is it that their 'knowing' is different, that in Bruner's terms it is within iconic or enactive modes of representation, and is not readily available within the symbolic mode. Or is it that the child sees this kind of exploration as irrelevant or uninteresting, or sees discussing matters such as these with an adult as inappropriate?

Although to anyone reading the transcriptions there are clear differences between the use of language by the advantaged and disadvantaged groups, it is not easy to find a means of comparison. The exploration had been designed to examine the extent to which children were able to offer explanations, and to discover how far they had moved towards logical thinking.

In the case of the advantaged groups, twelve children gave clear explanations that hinged on the *recognition of causal relationships*. Only six children in the disadvantaged groups adopted this kind of strategy and generally they succeeded in making fewer points. Seven children in the advantaged groups showed that they recognised each of the four basic relationships, whilst no child in the disadvantaged groups did this. The number of relationships recognised on average by the advantaged group was 3, whereas the children in the disadvantaged group averaged 1·8 of these relationships. There was no difference in the advantaged groups between boys and girls, but in the disadvantaged groups the mean score for the girls was 1·5 and for the boys 2·1. This difference seems unlikely to be because girls are less familiar with the action of these plastic bottles, although it may be that boys are more familiar with water pistol action, but this would seem likely to be so in the case of the advantaged groups also.

Chapter 12

Language and the Development of Moral Concepts

We have already agreed that Piaget has brought powerful evidence to show that conceptual thought arises from the child's operations on the elements of experience, upon the objects and their attributes, and upon inherent relationships that are transformed by his actions. Piaget agrees that language plays an important role in conceptual thinking, but argues:

... that thought precedes language and that language confines itself to profoundly transforming thought by helping it to attain its form of equilibrium by means of a more advanced schematisation and a more mobile abstraction. (Piaget, 1954)

It is quite clear that many basic concepts are derived directly from experience and are in no way dependent on language for their development. The hardness of 'hard' is a meaning that is based on the child's personal experiences that lead him to anticipate and avoid abrupt contact with hard objects. The labels that he learns to attach to such dominant aspects of his experiencing may do little to aid the development of the concept, although they will offer him ready means for communicating the notion to others.

Whilst it seems likely that the child would develop many lower order concepts without the help of language, it would also seem that higher order concepts, and those not readily gained from direct experience, are likely to be far more dependent on language for their development. The child is unable to form these higher order concepts, even though he may meet relevant experiences from which they could be abstracted, until his developing schemas make assimilation possible. Such concepts must await a necessary level of maturation, but the child's experiences contribute to the process of maturation, and amongst those experiences the language used by others plays its part in directing attention and placing experiences within a structure.

Amongst such concepts are those that relate to particular values held by the group. Values and judgements seem to be defined differently by different communities and societies, and differences in the children's values seem likely to result from the different viewpoints that the child hears expressed. Moral judgements would seem to lie within this category of higher order concepts, and we would predict that there would be differences between the groups in the development of moral judgements.

Piaget has provided a detailed study of children's development of moral judgements over a wide range of issues that are concerned with the way in which rules are recognised, applied and interpreted, and also with their view of transgressions (Piaget, 1932). He shows that, like other concepts, moral judgement develops sequentially and different bases of making judgements characterise different stages of development.

For the child to deal with moral issues, he requires particular ways of interpreting the effect of his own behaviour, and that of others, on other people. In school there is an assumption that children are able to make rational judgements, and that they are able to accept and understand the bases of 'acceptable', that is moral, behaviour.

To what extent are children, by the age of 7, able to make such judgements about behaviour, and are all children's values by the age of 7 developing in the same direction and at a similar rate? This was a question that it seemed would be useful for the study to explore as part of the attempt to investigate the way in which children's language is functioning to serve particular purposes. A problem was presented to the child in story form and then he was questioned about it.

* The story was introduced and told to the children as follows:

Introduction

Would you like to draw a picture today? Here is a story I want to tell you. Will you listen carefully because then I'd like you to draw me a picture about it with your friend? Are you ready?

The Story

Once upon a time there was a little white dog. He was called Spot because he had a big black spot on the end of his nose. Every day, Spot went to the butcher's shop at the end of the road because he wanted a bone, but every day the butcher chased Spot out. He didn't want any dogs in his shop. One day when Spot went to the butcher's shop, he saw that the butcher was very frightened. There was a bad man in the shop and he was stealing the butcher's money. The butcher couldn't get out. Spot barked very loudly and then bit the man's ankle. He kept his teeth there so that the man couldn't move. Then the butcher rushed outside and came back with a policeman, who took the bad man to the police station. The butcher was so pleased that he gave Spot a big juicy bone, and every day after that when Spot came into the shop, he got a bone.

This story was first used to see how well the child could repeat the story for the benefit of the friend who was to help him with drawing a picture. We shall discuss this activity in the following chapter.

* We are indebted to E. Garvie for suggesting the use of this story.

The child was first taken through the story again and then, before he invited his friend in to help him, he was asked the following questions:

1   Suppose it had been a little boy who had stolen the money, what would the butcher have done then?

This was followed by a supportive prompt, and then repetition of the question if the child did not answer readily.

2   Is it worse for a little boy to steal than it is for a big man?

This was followed by prompts according to the child's answer:

> What do you think? Is it worse? Why do you say that? Why is it worse for ——?

The story of Spot is modelled on stories used by Piaget in his examination of children's development of attitudes towards stealing and lying (Piaget, 1932, p. 116). In this work Piaget is seeking to examine the way in which the constraints imposed by adults on children's views of behaviour lead to the phenomenon of 'objective' responsibility. 'Objective responsibility' is the term applied to evaluations that are made in terms of the material results from a particular incident. 'Subjective responsibility', on the other hand, refers to evaluations that are based on the motives that lie behind particular incidents.

'Objective responsibility', according to Piaget, is characteristic of the child's thinking between the ages of 5 and 8 and stems from the child's acceptance of rules as things in themselves, eternal and unchanging, and springing from parental, or otherwise divine, authority. At this stage, a period referred to by Piaget as *transcendental*, the child recognises the rules or constraints but cannot keep them himself and he regards the extent of material damage as the main criterion by which transgressions should be judged. For example, in a story used by Piaget, children at the transcendental stage tend to judge the boy who breaks fifteen cups through an unavoidable accident as 'naughtier' than the one who accidentally breaks a a single cup whilst engaged in deliberate mischief.

The children at this stage regarded as most immoral those acts of stealing that had the most serious objective consequences, with no consideration of the subject's motives. Thus a child who steals a roll to give to a hungry person is judged guiltier than one who steals a ribbon for herself.

The children's responses to the issues raised by the story of Spot can be examined in the same way, although the bases of judgement were of a different kind. A subjective response in this case would seem to be a recognition that stealing was wrong for anyone, boy or man. If mitigation is considered, then a subjective response would compare the maturity and knowledge of the man with that of a small boy. A child may be considered too young to understand that it is wrong to steal, and therefore his intention would be seen to be of a different kind from that of a man who should know that it is an offence against other people.

Children's responses to this story fell into several categories. Only four children indicated explicitly that they understood that stealing was wrong whoever was the perpetrator. Their answers were as follows:

Andrew: Well . . . I think it's far, far worse for a man . . . a man should know that it's wrong to steal and that he'll go to prison and all that.
  The boy *should* know . . . but he might not realise that it's bad you know . . . er . . . but *he* might get sent away . . . boys sometimes do get sent away to a sort of school.
Joanna: Because a boy doesn't know and a man does know . . . but a man shouldn't steal nor should a little boy.
Fiona: Well little boys should not steal either . . . nobody should steal especially a man.

These three children were the only ones from the fifty-four children who were interviewed at this stage of the project who made explicit the principle that stealing is wrong whoever does it. They were all from the advantaged groups. Of the disadvantaged group, only Susan indicated the general rule 'You shouldn't steal money. The big man's worse than the little boy', but there was no justification given for her judgement.

But there were many who indicated implicitly that stealing was wrong, but who saw judgement, as it were, taking account of 'mitigating' circumstances. In this case importance was attached to the fact that young children might not understand why stealing is wrong, or blame might be placed on others, for example: 'His mother might not have told him that it's wrong to steal.' Examples of the responses of children who set this kind of meaning on the problem are the following:

Helen: I think it's worse for a man because . . . well the little boy might not know any better . . . perhaps he doesn't know cos no one's told him that it's wrong.
Neil: No it wouldn't be worse if a little boy did it . . . would it? A little boy might not know . . . his mother might not have told him not to do it. He couldn't go to prison could he? A boy would just get sent to bed for being so naughty.

Altogether ten children from the advantaged groups took the viewpoint that it was a matter of development or maturity, that is, that children have to learn that stealing is wrong but, by the time people are *older*, all should have learned that stealing is wrong. Only one other child, Gwen, from the disadvantaged group, looked at the problem from this viewpoint.

Gwen: A really big man is worst because he should not steal.
          Cos the little boy . . . I know . . .
          Cos the big man knows better but not the little boy.

Few of the 7-year-olds seemed able to see the problem as a matter of principle, that stealing is wrong and both man and boy should be censured. But the question itself can be seen to have some ambiguity. 'Supposing it had been a little boy stealing the money, would it be worse for him to steal than for the man?' The questioner assumes that 'worse' refers to the act of stealing, and we would expect that this assumption would be made by all adults. But if one has not yet learned the kind of reference such a question implies, then 'worse for a boy or a man' can be interpreted as leading to worse consequences for the man or the boy.

The difficulty can be seen as one of the development of meaning. The consequences no doubt relate to the meaning that 'stealing' has for the adult population as a whole: it is an anti-social act, condemned by the majority. But the meaning that 'stealing' has for the child is necessarily won by the child from the treatment of his own acts of taking things that do not belong to him, and from what he hears and sees others say and do about people who steal. Since he is not likely to learn about prison from his own direct experience, going to prison can only stem from the expressed views of others, and such vicarious experiences as are offered by film and television, and stories.

Perhaps the position taken up here corresponds to what Piaget has described as one of 'objective responsibility'. In this particular problem the amount of money stolen was not a central issue, but children centred their attention on the differences in the kind of punishment that boy and man might expect to receive. They were, then, concerned with the consequences of stealing rather than with stealing as an immoral act. The following are examples from responses that could be classified as instances of objective responsibility.

Mark: Because the boy is only taken home and the big burglar is taken to prison sometimes.
Sally: I think it's worser for a big man because I think they have to go to the police station . . . and a little boy . . . well . . . he might have got told off instead.
Stephen: Because a man goes to jail and *if* a boy does something wrong . . . naughty . . . he goes to a special school.

Andrew: Because if a little boy did it he'd only go to a naughty school but he wouldn't have to go to prison till he was old enough but a big man would.

These four were the only examples of 'objective responsibility' towards consequences that were offered by children from the advantaged groups and four children from the disadvantaged groups offered answers that had a similar basis.

Christopher: It's worse for a man because if they steal they get hanged or locked up in prison.

David: Because the boy wouldn't get sent to prison and his dad would.

Gary: The man ... because he can go to prison and the boy can't ... the boy could get sent away ... to a school but not a prison.

David: For a bad man ... because he'll go to jail and a little boy can't.

There were also two interesting examples from children in the advantaged groups that took a different view of consequences. These looked at what stealing in a child might lead on to, that is, the child might become an expert burglar, so that this was seen as of greater consequence than the fact that a man was already a burglar. Perhaps here is an example, in Piaget's term, of 'subjective responsibility', that is, that the intentions of a child might develop into persistent planned action.

Janet: Worse for the little boy ... because when he grows older he might become a worse stealer.

Andrew: Much worser for the little boy to steal because it means when the boy grows up he may learn ... he may start stealing all kinds of things.

These two responses, although not taking the expected position of judging the man to be the more guilty, are nevertheless accepted as indicating a reflectiveness and recognition of the general principle commensurate with those who argued from the position that a grown man has had plenty of time to learn and ought to know better.

A further group of responses is interesting because although they may not seem to be the most appropriate answers, nevertheless they can be seen to be a logical response to the question 'Which is worse?' Logically the answer can centre on (i) the crime – the expected mature interpretation, (ii) 'worse', which can be seen to direct attention to the consequences for the person involved, (iii) the problems for those who should apprehend the wrong-doer.

This last kind of imposition of meaning by the child was unexpected, but it was assumed by five of the advantaged group and two of the disadvantaged group, for example:

Tom: Worse if it's a big man, because he would have more ideas of escaping.

Simon: It's not worse if it's a boy because it will be easier to get him and a man will be . . . a grown man wouldn't be so easy to fight back against.

Joseph: Because a boy hasn't got a lot of chances but a man can . . . got a lot of chances cos he's bigger.
      If the butcher comes up to him the man can hit him and the boy can't do anything.

Q: So it's worse for the man to steal?

Joseph: Yes . . . if the butcher comes to him he could have hit him and then he could have got the money. The boy could run away but he wouldn't have no money.

Mark: Big man . . . because he can get all the money away and run off before anybody gets there . . . he gets out in time.

All the answers considered so far can be seen to stem from the child's attempts to put the incident into a logical framework. Altogether all but two of the advantaged group, that is twenty-two, were seeking interpretations that could be supported by logical argument. In comparison, only eight of the disadvantaged group approached the problem in this way, and most of these fell into the category of 'objective responsibility' towards consequences, that is, seeing the seriousness of the punishment as the most important aspect.

The remainder of the responses, two from the advantaged group, claimed that they were unable to judge, and sixteen from the disadvantaged group gave judgements that did not seem to stem from any logical basis.

Several children just stated that size was the important factor, for example:

Joanne: Because the little boy's little and the big man's big.

Other children made statements that avoided answering the question and, as it were, dismissed the subject as a matter for further consideration, for example:

Lynn: Because a big man is braver.

Richard: Because boys don't, don't . . . steal.
      Because big men have to be robbers and small boys can't be robbers.

Nicholas: Because a little boy wouldn't steal money because he wouldn't know how to do it.
Julie: Because he has no money.

In looking at many of these intuitive or pre-emptive answers, it seems likely that what the child expressed did not convey the full meaning that he could place on the incident, but rather that a prominent feature is selected to centre on and only this feature is expressed in words. There were, however, no examples where the child expanded his first response to give a more 'logical' answer when his first answer was echoed back to him.

On this question, then, it is clear that there are great differences in the meanings that are imposed by the advantaged and the disadvantaged groups. Twenty-two children from the advantaged group tried to place a logical structure upon their judgements and two were not prepared to make a judgement, saying they did not know whether it was worse for a man or a boy to steal. But two-thirds of the disadvantaged groups were not able, or were not disposed, to look for a logical framework in which to make their judgements.

Unlike concepts that are dependent on concrete, direct, sensory experience for their establishment, moral concepts would seem to depend to a large extent on the kind of interpretation that is laid upon them by others. It might be argued that the concept grows from the treatment of children's own misdemeanours and the punishments meted out to them, and that this serves as direct experience and concrete example. But we can see that what people say at the time may influence the child's view of the situation. It must be true that there is a limit to the child's understanding, and perhaps this is illustrated by the number of children in the advantaged groups who perhaps were developing the kind of strategies needed for the interpretation at a level of the application of principles, but who had not yet been able to recognise the crucial feature from a number of other factors that intruded.

Explanations offered by parents and others of the basis of moral behaviour may have to await a maturing of the child's ability to abstract general principles. Where children meet no explanations of this kind, but where punishment is seen as the major consequence of his, and others', transgressions, then the child is left to make what sense he can of the causal relationship between his behaviour and his punishment.

Perhaps this is an area where the experiences that the child meets of the interpretations set on situations by others is of paramount importance. It is an area in which it can be seen that what is said to the child, and the way in which values are consistently expressed, lead to very different interpretations of situations that are familiar to all children. Meanings of experiences such as these are changed by what is said to the child. The linguistic experience modifies the child's reception of his direct experiencing. We might then ask to what extent it is the strategies induced by the language experiences that lead to the child's ability to develop moral concepts and what the implications of this must be if Kohlberg is right in saying:

Only as children reach a level of cognitive development at which the meaning of moral concepts can be differentiated from punishment can they attain either a definite hedonism or a degree of disinterested respect for authority. (Kohlberg, 1963, p. 22)

Perhaps it leads us to see, why as Kohlberg indicates, internal moral standards are the outcome of a 'set of transformations of primitive attitudes and conceptions' rather than a process of 'stamping in' the external prohibitions of the culture upon the child's mind. (Ibid., p. 11)

To what extent are transformations accomplished by the assimilation of attitudes and strategies developed by the child through his experiences of language used by and with others? Perhaps, we should again consider the part that what is said to the young child about his everyday experiencing plays in helping the child to become aware of, and set a structure upon, the phenomena he is continually faced with.

Chapter 13

Language and Disadvantage in School

The main purpose of this book has been to give some account of the exploratory work of the longitudinal study of the development of language. In doing this we have tried to give a picture of the children's responses and to examine the problems that have emerged and the implications that might be drawn from the results.

Throughout the discussion we have used the terms *advantaged* and *disadvantaged* to refer to the children in the selected groups. It is important to remember, however, that at the time of selection the individual children in the study were 3 years old and there was no evidence to show that as individuals they were either at advantage or disadvantage within education, for they had not yet started in the infants' school. Nor was there any justification for predicting from general observations of these 3-year-olds that they would respond differently to their experiences in school.

We must remind the reader that all the children selected for the study at the age of 3 were friendly and talkative, and all were of average intelligence, or above, on a Stanford Binet Test of Intelligence. The description of the groups as advantaged or disadvantaged, then, was not derived from any demonstrated characteristic of the children in the groups. The children were allocated to the groups on the basis of the proven advantage or disadvantage of the section of the population to which their parents belonged.

Our aim was to study differences in the use of language that emerged that might be expected to affect children's responses to their school experiences.

How then did the children fare? Did they fulfil the development that might have been predicted from their measured intelligence or from their social class origins? And what role did language play in shaping the responses that they were able to make to their school experiences?

The Child's Progress in School

At each stage of the study, information was gathered on each child's general progress in school. Since children had been selected who were generally friendly and socially well-adjusted at the outset it might be expected that there would be few serious problems of adjustment to school. But situations change for children, and in four years apparently stable homes, under different kinds of pressure, can become less stable. This had happened in a number of cases, and the effects on children were reported by their teachers. Nevertheless they remained on the whole well-adjusted to school although there were some differences between the advantaged and the disadvantaged groups.

All the children in the advantaged groups were, in their teachers' views well-adjusted in school. One child was known to be considerably disturbed at home, and at school was seen as needing to assert himself and he was sometimes aggressive and a nuisance. One girl at 5 caused her teacher some anxiety because at first she seemed over-anxious and shy. However, this had quickly disappeared and at the age of 7 she was considered to be a leader within the class.

In the disadvantaged groups three boys and two girls were reported to have serious problems in school. It was reported that one girl was taking other children's possessions and being spiteful and aggressive. The second girl was known to have been seriously abused at home and in school was reported to be apprehensive but having no problems with either teachers or children. One of the boys was reported to be very stubborn in class, refusing to talk to the teacher, and unable to maintain good relationships with children. A second boy was reported as being already well on the way to being delinquent. His older brothers were in considerable trouble with the police and this child was expected to follow in the same way. The child's mother and the school had very different views of this child and very different explanations for his behaviour. The third boy was reported to be very anxious in school, and had been moved from his first school because his mother felt he was not getting on well. Apart from these seven children, however, all the children were reported by their teachers as well-adjusted to school.

When we looked at how the children were progressing in reading the picture was different. Watts Sentence Reading Test was used to test the children's ability in reading. This test is intended for children between the ages of 7 years and 6 months and 11 years and 1 month. It is a test in which the child reads incomplete sentences and chooses one word, from five alternatives, to complete the sentence. Thus it is a test of comprehension also. Because the children were known to be of average or above average intelligence it was expected that a test of this kind would be most suitable for discriminating amongst them. However, it demands that the child has developed some skill in reading before he can score at all.

The children in the advantaged groups generally responded well to the test. Several read through much of the test quickly and accurately in the allotted time. All had established skill that was at least commensurate with their age, and all but two scored over 110. (The test is standardised to a score of 100 with a standard deviation of 15.) These two children were seen by their teachers as having difficulties, although they had scores of 105 and 108. The teachers' concern for these two children, one a girl and the other a boy, was that they were not reading as well as might be expected from their general background and observed ability in other areas of learning.

The results for the disadvantaged groups, however, were very different. Five girls and three boys had scores above 110, but the majority were scoring around and below the 100 level. Four boys were not able to score anything on this test, although all, in their teachers' views, had begun to read. In retrospect, a different test might have demonstrated better what these children had achieved.

We are well aware of the problems of testing reading, particularly of finding suitable tests to use with children who have learned by different methods and are familiar with a different range of vocabulary. Since the children were in a number of schools, the problems were common to both the advantaged and the disadvantaged group and the only purpose of using a reading test was to discriminate between the groups, and to give some indication of the relative progress of the groups. From their performances on this test the children in the advantaged groups were well ahead, with a mean score of 118, and on the whole were fulfilling the potential indicated by their estimated IQs. The majority of children in the disadvantaged groups had made less progress, and from their mean score of 103 were doing less well than would be expected from evidence of their intelligence scores.

Measured Intelligence of the Groups

At the outset of the study we had been anxious that any differences that appeared between the groups of children should not be explained by differences in intelligence. For this reason we had not included any child in the study who had an IQ of less than 105 on the Stanford Binet Test of Intelligence. The mean IQs of the groups of 3-year-old children selected for the study were at the outset 126·3 and 124·1 for the advantaged groups and disadvantaged groups respectively.

We are aware of the problems of assessing children's intelligence at so early an age, and of placing reliance on it, but the assessments were made in an effort to ensure that we had some justification for making comparisons. The generally lower IQs of all the children at the age of 5, shown in Table 6 in the Appendix, p. 192 was unexpected and seems likely to be due mainly to the use of different tests. The Wechsler Intelligence Scale for Children was used to assess intelligence when the children were $5\frac{1}{2}$ and $7\frac{1}{2}$. Since WISC is not designed to use with children under the age of 5, it was not possible to use it for the first assessments. But WISC was preferred to Stanford Binet since it is made up of verbal and performance scales and this seemed likely to provide useful information.

Many studies have found high correlation between the Stanford Binet and the WISC scales. Butcher reviews these studies and indicates that they would seem to have about 80 per cent of variance in common (Butcher, 1968). However, Stanford Binet has been found systematically to give higher results throughout the range, and in addition WISC has been found to be capable of less discrimination at higher levels, so that generally lower IQs for all the children at $5\frac{1}{2}$ years old seems likely to be due mainly to the use of the two different scales. The mean IQ for the disadvantaged groups was lower than for the advantaged groups, however. The estimated mean IQs using WISC were at this stage 116·3 and 122·1 respectively, and the estimated differences between the verbal and the performance scale were greater for the disadvantaged groups than for the advantaged groups.

At the age of $7\frac{1}{2}$ the picture is similar: although the advantaged group has maintained the mean IQ, the mean IQ of the disadvantaged group is almost four points lower. At this age the groups have mean IQs of 121·3 and 112·4 and the differences between scores on the verbal scale and on the performance scale are greater for the disadvantaged group than for the advantaged group.

We see, then, a general picture of lowering IQ for children from the unskilled and semi-skilled section of the population as they get older, although there were a few untypical results. This is a pattern that has been seen in other studies, for example, in the large-scale survey by Douglas (Douglas, 1964). In the present study the fall is larger than that observed by others but since the children in the selected groups were all above average IQ, some fall would be expected from regression to the mean. Whatever the cause of the lowering IQ, it is clear that by the age of $7\frac{1}{2}$ children in the disadvantaged groups had already revealed their disadvantage in school. Not only did they tend to do less well on the reading test than children whose parents were in professions, but also their measured ability on intelligence tests was lower at the age of $7\frac{1}{2}$. We shall return to a discussion of this question at a later point.

Throughout this book we have discussed the differences that have been found between the groups in the language recorded at three ages. Several studies have assumed that there is a causal relationship between the child's knowledge of, and ability to use, language and his progress in school, and programmes have been designed to make good the apparent deficit. We will summarise now the differences in the use of language that were identified between the groups during the study.

A Summary of Differences in the Use of Language

Although we would not claim that we have found entirely satisfactory ways of gaining representative samples of children's language or of analysing them, we feel that the methods we have used have provided insights into the nature of the differences that were developing between the children in the groups drawn from different sections of the population.

When the children were 5 and 7 we had devised situations that aimed at taking a closer view of the way in which they were able to use language for particular purposes. Those purposes under investigation corresponded with the main functions of language that we had recognised in the talk of 3-year-olds, and the intention was to consider the development of these functions and to identify any differences between the groups of children in the kind of strategies they seemed disposed to use in fulfilling these functions.

From the discussion in the last three chapters we can see that clear differences emerged between the groups of children in the kinds of strategies used as they:

1 interpreted pictures of ongoing scenes;
2 recalled past experiences;
3 projected through the imagination into the possibilities of imagined situations;
4 explained a process and reasoned about problems;
5 made judgements about behaviour.

In earlier chapters the differences between the children in the advantaged and disadvantaged groups in the way in which language was used to meet these tasks have been identified and discussed. The children in the advantaged groups tended to elaborate a wider range of meaning than children in the disadvantaged groups on all the tasks considered so far. In some tasks the kinds of interpretations that children were able to impose were clearly of a different order. There were variations *within* the groups so that neither mean performance nor the cumulative picture can be said to represent *typical* performances. The methods of functional analysis that were used, however, allowed comparisons to be made between the groups on the incidence of particular strategies. The value of the functional analysis lies, perhaps, in the insights that it provides when inferences are being drawn from more objective data. This is the case in this study. Linguistic indices were used as the basis of comparison at each age level, but the inferences that we draw from these are not the same as they would have been had the results of the functional analysis not been available.

Most prominent in the current debate on the part played by language in learning and in communication is the role of linguistic structure in conveying meaning. Bernstein, for example, puts forward a theory that places emphasis on the characteristic linguistic feature of the talk typical of particular sections of the population, and sees these differences as having an importance for the child's learning. Others, for example Labov and

Rosen, have challenged the view that differences of this kind are important (Labov, 1970; Rosen, 1972). Labov seeks to show that American black youths who use non-standard English are nevertheless communicating at least as well as those from the middle class who speak standard English.

What is the issue at stake in this argument? It is not so much an argument about whether the differences in the surface structure of the language used by different sections of the community occur or not; a great amount of research now exists to witness that there are differences in the forms of the language used by children from different sections of the population. What is being questioned is whether the differences are of any importance for learning and for benefiting from experiences in school. What can we infer from our examination of linguistic features, and how do the differences identified relate to our knowledge of the way in which the children *used* language?

In the present study all the recorded responses of the children at the three ages have been subjected to both a linguistic and a functional analysis. The linguistic measures that were used to compare the language used by groups of 3-year-olds have been discussed in Chapters 2 and 3. They include the mean length of all utterances, the noun phrase index, the verb phrase index, a classification of the complexity of all utterances, and a measure of the use of the pronoun, referred to as the reference index. The table below shows the mean score for each group on three of these measures at the three different ages.

It can be seen from this table that as children grow older their utterances tend to be longer. The increase in length is, in part at least, due to the fact

Mean score for groups at three ages

	M.U. length		Noun phrase Index		Verb phrase Index	
	Adv.	Disadv.	Adv.	Disadv.	Adv.	Disadv.
At 3: girls	5·8	4·0	2·2	2·0	4·4	3·2
boys	5·8	3·9	2·3	2·0	4·3	3·4
all	5·8	4·0	2·3	2·0	4·4	3·3
At 5: girls	6·8	4·9	2·6	2·4	4·6	3·8
boys	6·3	4·4	2·5	2·3	4·7	3·7
all	6·6	4·7	2·6	2·4	4·7	3·8
At 7: girls	9·9	7·7	2·5	2·4	5·2	4·8
boys	10·1	7·8	2·6	2·3	4·9	4·5
all	10·0	7·7	2·6	2·4	5·1	4·7

that as children grow older they tend towards greater elaboration of the noun phrase, and greater extension of the verb phrase.

We can see from this table that the differences between the advantaged and the disadvantaged groups are maintained throughout the four years. These figures do not, however, indicate the variations that there are in the scores *within* groups, but there was in fact little overlap in scores between the advantaged and disadvantaged groups on any of the measures; using a ranking test the differences between the groups on these measures are found to be significant at least at the 0·05 level and on some measures at a level of 0·001. These results confirm what others have discovered, that children of middle-class parents tend to show higher scores on linguistic measures than children from lower-working-class parents, but we must consider carefully the interpretation that should be set on these differences. What inferences can be drawn from the results of the analyses?

Some Problems of Making Inferences from Linguistic Data

Some of the problems of making inferences can be illustrated by examining the results from the analysis of linguistic data further.

When the children were 7 a series of tasks was presented to them, including those that have already been described. Three situations used have not yet been described. The first of these looked at the child's ability to reproduce language that had been, as it were, 'given' to him. The story of Spot, given on page 142, was told to the child, and before he and his friend settled down to draw a picture he was asked to retell the story to his friend. His ability to produce long utterances using complex structures, even if they were a repetition of utterances heard earlier, meant that he had the resources that allowed him to produce complex forms. It seemed unlikely that the child who was able to repeat the story, making agreements and using conjunctions, giving the detail and sequence, could do so without adequate resources.

A second task was designed to examine the child's ability to give explicit instructions to another. This task used a range of shapes cut from vinyl tiles of different sizes and different colours. There were large and small squares, rectangles, triangles and circles, each in red, green, blue, yellow and white. Pictures of a ship, a house and a railway engine had been made from a similar set of shapes cut in sticky paper. The pictures could be reproduced using the vinyl shapes by following the organisation of shapes in the pictures.

The child and two of his friends sat at a table; the interviewer first played the role of instructor so that the children might learn what was expected of them. Without letting the child see the picture, the interviewer took the ship picture and began to give instructions to the two children

about making the picture. For example: first take the large yellow rectangle, and place it in the centre of the paper but only a little way from the
bottom edge. Now take a small yellow triangle and put it at one end of the
rectangle, to make the back of the boat. Take another yellow triangle and
place it in the same way at the other end of the rectangle, to make the
front of the ship.

The two children made their picture, interpreting and following directions the interviewer had given. The child who was not in the selected
sample then took the picture of the house and gave the child in the study
instructions about building this from the vinyl shapes. Finally the child in
the study took over the role of instructor and directed his friend in making
the third picture.

The essential condition of this activity was that the child could not see
what the other was doing in response to the instructing and was expected
to see that his description needed to be clear and explicit.

The third situation still to be reported was the child's conversations
with his friend, which were recorded at two points in the interview. The
first occasion followed the child's reproduction of the story of Spot, when
the child invited his friend to draw a picture with him. When the children
had settled to draw a picture together, the interviewer made an excuse to
leave the room, suggesting that the children worked together to finish the
picture. The tape recorder was left running until the observer returned.

The second conversation was collected in a similar manner. When the
child had finished instructing his friend to make a picture with the vinyl
shapes, it was suggested that they might now like to make some pictures of
their own from the shapes and again an excuse was made to leave the room
and the tape recorder was left running.

These three situations produced (1) a repeated story, (2) the child's
directions to his friend to use the shapes to make the picture and (3) two
conversations between the child and his friend, and completed the language
data that were collected from the children at the age of $7\frac{1}{2}$.

SOME CONTRADICTIONS

The table below gives the results of the linguistic analyses that were applied
to the collected data.

What is the picture of the disadvantaged child that emerges from
examining this table?

First of all, it is clear that on nearly all measures the mean scores for the
disadvantaged group are less than those for the advantaged group. For all
the activities except free conversations the disadvantaged children's utterances tend to be considerably shorter than those of the advantaged
children. The advantaged group are clearly using longer and perhaps more
complex utterances, and saying considerably more about the situation than

the disadvantaged group. The difference holds in the same direction for the noun phrase index, but the position is reversed in the case of the verb phrase index where in three situations the mean score for the disadvantaged is as high as or higher than that of the advantaged.

	Mean utterance length		Mean No. words		Noun phrase index		Verb phrase Index	
	Adv.	Disadv.	Adv.	Disadv.	Adv.	Disadv.	Adv.	Disadv.
Bus picture (interpretation)	8·6	5·6	164	108	2·5	2·4	4·7	4·7
Picture outlines (projection)	8·3	5·5	48·7	19	2·3	2·2	4·2	4·5
Squirter (causal explanation)	8·5	5·4	84·6	52·8	2·5	1·9	3·5	3·5
Tile picture (instructing)	7·6	6·3	172	165	3·7	3·9	1·5	1·6
Story repetition	14	10	127	100				
Free conversations	5·1	5·1					2·4	2·1

What should we infer from this analysis? It might seem that the advantaged children just talked more than the disadvantaged: this conclusion is a justifiable one, although of course it cannot be said that every one of the advantaged children said more during the interviews than every one of the disadvantaged children. This is not quite the case, but the advantaged children generally produced more in their first responses and said more in response to subsequent prompts than the disadvantaged children. But we can see that the difference between the two groups was greater when imaginative projection was asked for. Here the number of words produced by the children in the disadvantaged groups was less than half that produced by the children in the advantaged groups.

The mean length of utterance for children in the disadvantaged groups is also interesting. Whilst it remains low beside the advantaged groups, we can see that when repeating the story the mean length of utterances is almost twice as high as for other situations. But in this situation the mean length of utterances for the disadvantaged group is higher than the mean length for the advantaged group in any of the other situations.

We could also infer from the table that the disadvantaged children used fewer adjectives and adjectival phrases than the advantaged group; this is reflected in the differences in the Noun Phrase Index. But here too there are contradictions, for in the picture-constructing activity the mean index for the disadvantaged groups is higher than that of the advantaged groups.

Are we justified, then, in saying that the disadvantaged children have a language deficit and need to be taught more about using language? Or should we infer that the difference between the groups is just that the children in the advantaged groups are more verbose? The functional analysis indicated that it was precisely those uses that were thought to reflect complex thinking that more frequently appeared in the talk of the children in the advantaged groups: little was revealed that could be described as 'just talk'; all talk was purposeful, even though it was not all at a level of adult thinking.

So is it that the disadvantaged children have less knowledge than the advantaged children about using language? Can the view that the disadvantaged child is limited to the use of short utterances be sustained?

Although it is true that the mean length of utterance is generally shorter for the disadvantaged group than for the advantaged group, we need to look at the range in the length of utterances before drawing conclusions. In the story repetition situation, for example, the mean length of utterances for the children in the disadvantaged groups is almost twice the mean length of the utterances produced in the free conversations. In the story-telling activity the children heard utterances sequenced in narrative form, and they showed that they could reproduce the story using many of the original features. In this situation the children in the disadvantaged group extended the verb as required by the story, and elaborated the noun to give description, and used clauses. Although the mean length of their utterances is not nearly so long as those of the advantaged groups, it is clear that the disadvantaged children were able to reproduce much of what they had heard. In the original story twelve utterances (in this case sentences) were used. The advantaged groups retold the story using an average of nine utterances, whilst the disadvantaged groups used ten.

The original story used 163 words. This was reduced to an average of 127 in the stories told by the advantaged groups and to 100 in the stories retold by the disadvantaged groups. The mean length of the utterances in the original story was 13·5: this increased to 14 when the story was retold by children in the advantaged groups and reduced to 10 when retold by the children in the disadvantaged group. But there is no doubt that all the children showed that they were able to retain the essential features of the story and to use very much the same form of utterances as the original. The following are three examples from the disadvantaged group:

Susan: There was a white dog that had a big spot on its nose.
It went to the butcher's . . . and the butcher chased it out.
Then the next day he went and the butcher was very

       frightened . . . because . . . er . . . there was a man stealing
       the money.
        And he bit his ankle and kept hold of it with his teeth.
       And the butcher went out and brought a policeman back
       And the policeman took him to the police station.
       He gave him a bone every day.

David: There were this dog.
       And his name were called Spot 'cos he had a right big
       spot on back . . . on front of his nose.
        And every day dog went to't butcher's and he wanted a
       bone . . .
       and butcher didn't give him one.
       Next day he went and . . . and . . . and he went to butcher's
       and butcher shooed him out of shop 'cos he wouldn't give
       him it.
        Next day the butcher were right frightened.
       There were a bad man and he were stealing all his money.
       And Spot came in and . . . and he got hold of his ankle
       and t'butcher ran out and got a policeman . . . um . . .
       and then . . . and then . . . er . . .
       the butcher gave him big juicy bone and every time Spot
       came he gave him a bone.

Christopher: There was a man and he was a butcher
       And he would not give the dog a bone
       'Cos he didn't like that dog.
        And one day there was a murderer and he took the
       butcher's money and he took . . .
        The dog caught his leg and he wouldn't let go . . .
       so he gave it a bone every day.

  Christopher's story reproduction was the shortest and one that omitted
a number of the story points. However, even though the story had been
considerably reduced, it still retained much of the original.

  A tendency seen in the advantaged group was to reduce the number of
words needed, by using words with concentrated meaning, for example
'Spot defended the butcher' or 'Spot attacked the robber'. Perhaps this
is an indication of a development towards the use of concise expressions.
There was no evidence of such a development in the stories retold by the
children in the disadvantaged groups.

  The children in the disadvantaged groups show that they have adequate
resources of language for this activity since they were able to remember
sequences and reproduce the story line, including much of the detail. Yet
if we look again at the table we can see that the scores for retelling a story
are not typical of their performances in other situations. We cannot make

statements about children's use of language that hold for any and every situation. We must look, then, at the kind of demands that are being made in different contexts in order to understand why there should be such great differences in children's performances between one situation and another.

The Noun Phrase Index in four different situations can be taken as an example. The mean score on the Noun Phrase Index for the disadvantaged group ranged from 1·9 to 3·7 and is quite close to those for the advantaged groups except in one situation. The exception is in the task that required causal explanations for the squirter action of the plastic bottle, when the scores on the Noun Phrase Index are 2·5 for the advantaged groups and 1·9 for the disadvantaged groups. The 'squirter' situation involved a concrete situation in which the pronoun could be used effectively for reference. Although the use of the pronoun was a characteristic feature of the disadvantaged child's performance, it does not affect scores on the Noun Phrase Index. But because it is a concrete situation it may seem unnecessary to give descriptive information. In the typical script from the disadvantaged group given below, there are no adjectives used with the nouns, but also the articles are omitted, so reducing the score for each noun phrase.

Linda: You push *bottle* in like this . . .
squeeze it and . . .
let *water* go into it.
And then you bring it up out of *water*
and it's flat like that . . .
and then
squeeze it like that and it comes back.
And you squirt *water* out.

Using an index where article, adjective and noun score equally, the child who omits the articles must produce low scores. But this omission is typical of the talk of the adult population in the areas in which the children live and cannot be seen as failure to learn. But in this situation, where most noun phrases are likely to consist of article and a noun with plural agreements when necessary, the child who consistently omits articles, and scores less, may be judged to be communicating less effectively, when this may not be the case. The inferences drawn from linguistic measures may therefore be unjustified.

In the instructional task the mean score on the Noun Phrase Index for the disadvantaged group stands at 3·9 and is higher than that of the advantaged group, which stands at 3·7. What interpretation should be set on this? How can the position be so reversed? This does not seem to be consistent with the characteristic behaviour of the children in the disadvantaged group.

The reversal of the scores of the disadvantaged and the advantaged groups occurred in the situation in which the child was instructing his friend to use the vinyl shapes to construct a picture.

For the majority of children this was a frustrating situation because they were unable to see what the other child was doing. Normally in such an activity they would be pointing, and demonstrating, as they used pronouns 'Get that one, and put it there like that'. In concrete situations where everyone can see what is going on, communication is not entirely dependent on the words used. When the child is separated from the visual display by a screen, or by distance, we have a situation in which explicitness is demanded where it is not normally needed. Some children could not restrain their frustration in this situation and could not be restrained from looking over the screen. All in the end, however, were able to accept the required information could be given in their instructions. Some children were much more successful than others in giving instructions that the other child could follow and that led to the intended construction. The following two examples illustrate this point:

Example 1

David: Take a red oblong . . . put in the left side.

    Take a green square and put in on the right side of the red oblong.

    Get a green wheel and put it underneath the red oblong.

    Get that white strip . . . take a white wheel . . . put that white strip on to the green wheel.

    Get a red wheel . . . I don't know what they call them. I've forgotten.

Observer: Rectangle.

David: No . . . oblong . . . a little oblong. Get a big red square . . . get a red wheel – put it under the square red block . . . get a white oblong . . . put it on top of the green square . . . get a green oblong . . . put it on top of the white oblong pointing to the right hand.

    Get a white square . . . put it on top of the red block. Get a green oblong . . . put it on top of the red square . . . on your left-hand side.

    Now . . . what is it?

Example 2

Alan: Are you ready now? We'll start at the right . . . no your left-side of the paper, about an inch and about three inches from the bottom . . . right?

Simon: OK – what do I put there?

Alan: Get the big red rectangle and put it there . . . short side
upwards . . .ready?

Take the little green rectangle and put it standing up
above the red rectangle a bit to the left . . . and then
put a little white square just behind it.

Simon: Wait a minute . . . right?

Alan: Now find a big green square and put it on the right of
the red one . . . level at the bottom . . . got it?

Now stand a little white square . . . on top of . . . no inside
the green square . . . near the top . . . about the middle.

And the little green rectangle across the top of the
green square.

Now you want big wheels under that . . . green one at the
front and white one at the back and a white strip across the
two rounds . . . how's that?

Some children were much more capable than others when giving
instructions about positioning the pieces. Alan, for example, projects into
the problem of the other child and gives not only information about the
location but also about the orientation of the piece. The children in the
advantaged groups produced twice as many instructions about positioning
the pieces as the children in the disadvantaged groups. All the children
described the pieces effectively, however, and the disadvantaged groups
had a higher mean score for the noun phrase than the advantaged groups.

In this situation, then, the disadvantaged children showed that they
could elaborate the noun phrase very effectively when the task demanded
it. They made efforts to be explicit in a situation in which explicitness was
not generally needed. When they saw the need for explicitness and were
motivated to make the necessary effort, they had the resources from which
to construct elaborate noun phrases.

In another situation the mean score on the verb index is higher for the
disadvantaged group than for the advantaged group. This occurs in the
task in which explanation of why a squeezy bottle makes a good squirter is
asked for. Why should the disadvantaged child elaborate more in this
situation than the advantaged child? The following two examples illustrate
the kind of strategies that led to this result. The first example is typical of
the advantaged groups.

Alan: This thing *has squashy* sides, *see*? So when you *squeeze* it you *send*
out all the air. Then you *put* the end, the hole under the water and
let the squashy sides *go* . . . then gradually the sides *come* out and
the water *is pulled* in . . . like that. Then you *squeeze* again and the
water *is forced* out through the hole. It *makes* a good water
pistol . . . only *it's* a bit too big.

The second example shows ways of extending the verb that were typical of the disadvantaged child's efforts in this situation.

Nigel: You*'ve got to squeeze* it like that . . . and you*'ve got to press* the air out. Then the water *has to get* in. And you*'ve got to lift* it out and you*'ve to squeeze* it and it *comes squirting out*.

Here we can see that because Alan took up an explanatory form 'so when you *squeeze*', 'then gradually the sides *come* out' he adopts generalising forms that can, as it were, be detached from the concrete situation. This tended to be the kind of strategy used by the children in the advantaged groups.

Nigel, however, sees the situation as one in which the rules are laid down and uses the strategy 'you*'ve got* to' as he demonstrates the squirter in use.

It cannot be claimed, perhaps, that either form serves the particular purpose any better than the other, although we might take it that the *meaning* of the task is perhaps different for the two boys. But, if neither is better, then 'superiority' must not be read into the longer mean verb index. Using 'got to' or 'have to' at every verb point increases the score for each verb complex, which is quite unjustified in terms of meaning.

From these examples it is clear that we ought to be very cautious about the way in which linguistic data are interpreted. Higher mean scores do not necessarily reflect more extensive meaning. Low scores in some situations do not necessarily mean that the child would have low scores in all situations. Nor should we take it that because the child makes low mean scores he is unable to make elaborations when he finds it appropriate to do so.

One of the most important aspects of the linguistic indices is that although generally the disadvantaged children show lower mean scores for all measures, the range of scores is not necessarily less. Although the disadvantaged children have a lower mean score for the verb index, they all use some verb phrases that have high scores. It is not that they never use high scoring verb phrases, but that they use them less frequently than the advantaged children. Although the disadvantaged children have a lower mean score for the noun phrase than the advantaged children at times, as we have seen, they use high scoring noun phrases. Although on most tasks the mean length of utterances for the disadvantaged children was lower than for the advantaged children, nevertheless all the children produced long complex utterances at times. When they engaged in conversation with a friend, the mean score for the length of utterances was the lowest for any situation and was the same for both advantaged and disadvantaged groups. But within these conversations, some of the longest and most complex utterances were used by the disadvantaged children as well as by the advantaged. For example:

If you get to play out tonight have we to go and do some more logging for the bonfire 'cos if we don't it won't be as big as Kingy's lot.

Our Mandy's going to get me when I get home 'cos I had a ride on her bike 'cos my mam said I could if I didn't go off street and I didn't because she wouldn't have let me have it again if I'd gone off.

These are two utterances produced by disadvantaged children. They are long and complex because of the ideas that are being expressed and because they refer away from the concrete present situation they need to be explicit. What is the motivation for being explicit in these two examples? Each refers to the child's own involvement in something that matters a great deal to him. In each case he is concerned to maintain his own self-interest. In the spontaneous conversations with their friends the longest utterances recorded by the disadvantaged groups all came within this use of language.

What inferences about the disadvantaged child's use of language are we justified in making? In this chapter we have tried to illustrate the dangers of interpreting results that are obtained when linguistic measures are used without making a closer examination of the demands of the situations in which the language samples were gathered. We have tried also to show that inferences that might be drawn from a comparison of *mean* performance may not be justified when consideration is given to the range of the child's performances.

When we consider the evidence from out study in this way, it would seem that the generally lower scores made by the children in the disadvantaged groups cannot be explained by their failure to develop complex forms of language, or by their lack of vocabulary, or by an inability to elaborate the noun phrase and extend the verb phrase. All the children in the disadvantaged groups showed that they could at times make long utterances, elaborate the noun phrase, extend the verb phrase and forsake pronouns in favour of nouns. The lower scores of the children in the disadvantaged groups would seem to be explained more satisfactorily by the kind of view that the child seemed to take of his experiences. This view is one that does not impose the same kind of structure and complex meaning on events and situations as children who are at advantage. The disadvantaged children are not inclined to reflect on the meaning of their own experiences, or to project readily into the experiences of others. They do not give explanations and justifications readily, nor do they reflect readily on past experiences, injecting them into the present to illuminate understanding. Nor do they anticipate the future readily and plan and consider alternative possibilities. But it would seem that it is not necessarily a lack of resources of language that governs what they do. The child's disadvantage in school seems to stem more from a lack of motivation to think in these ways, from lack of experience of thinking in these ways and from his general lack of awareness of meanings of this kind.

We perhaps should consider again the inferences that we are justified in drawing from the drop in measured IQs of children in the disadvantaged group, between the ages of 3 and 7, shown in Table 6 in the Appendix, page 192. At the age of 3 the children were generally friendly, talkative and confident since these had been necessary conditions for obtaining representative samples of their talk and were therefore used as criteria for selecting them for study. They scored well on the vocabulary items, were able to follow instructions and were generally curious and eager to manipulate the concrete materials offered to them for the test items. But other elements enter into WISC and children are asked to give explanations, to reflect and give judgements. Is it possible that the fall in IQ for children in the disadvantaged groups is in part due to the different expectations of children in these groups towards the test situation itself and in their interpretation of the problems put to them?

What assumptions do we make when we give tests? First of all, tests assume that all children will take the same view of questions and will be similarly motivated to answer. The instructions for carrying out WISC make clear that the test should be administered in a manner that allows good rapport to be established. But even where the tester's relationships with children are good, it would seem that there are differences between children in their expectations about answering questions. This was very evident in the study. For example, children in the disadvantaged groups tended to respond with 'I don't know' or avoid answering the question by offering some remark that seemed unrelated or tangential to the question asked. Frequently it was found that when children's first efforts were supported and they were helped to discover what was expected, they demonstrated that they had considerable resources from which to answer. When WISC is administered, however, no guidance is given for dealing with 'I don't know' or avoidance responses. Presumably they are to be judged as failing the question. Testers are warned that only neutral inquiry should be used; for example, the tester is recommended to follow up only when he is not sure whether the subject knows the meaning of a word or whether an answer shows adequate knowledge.

From the experience of the project, when the designed questions and follow-up prompts had been given and then a further exploration was undertaken to discover whether the child had a basis for answering the question appropriately or not, many children who had rejected the question, or who had given short evasive or inadequate answers, showed that the problem was not so much lack of knowledge but was due to something that might be described as lack of appropriate expectations or lack of awareness of what they knew. They were not disposed, it seemed, to search for, or recognise, information that they held as appropriate for answering the questions put to them.

We might ask, then, to what extent such attitudes or dispositions are operating within the individual test situation. The results can be seen as a measure of the child's ability to respond to questions asked in the test situation, but the results may be an underestimate of his knowledge and understanding. It is possible, then, that the drop in IQ is at least in part a reflection of already established dispositions towards dealing with questions and of his lack of practice in reflecting and drawing upon his inner resources. In other words, his responses to tests may be an indication of interpretations of his experiences that are now well established and set him at disadvantage within school.

Chapter 14

The Development of Meaning

Children's Knowledge of Language

In this final chapter we must consider the inferences that might be drawn from the evidence of the longitudinal study. What have we learned about the disadvantaged child's knowledge and use of language that might have implications for the way in which we approach his problems in school? What are the implications of our findings for early childhood education?

We must first consider whether there is evidence from the study to support the view that children from the unskilled and semi-skilled section of the population are at disadvantage within education because they have failed to develop adequate resources of language. The children in the disadvantaged groups scored less than the children in the advantaged groups on all measures of linguistic structure. These children used explicitness or elaboration less frequently than the children in the advantaged groups. They used pronouns instead of nouns more frequently, and they used adjectives and extensions of the verbs to future, conditional and past tenses less frequently than the children in the advantaged groups. None of the evidence, however, indicates that they used pronouns because they did not know the nouns that they replaced or that they did not describe detail because they did not know the relevant adjectives. And although they extended the verb less frequently than children in the advantaged groups this was not because they did not know how to use auxiliaries and modals. Although the children in the disadvantaged groups tended to use fewer complex utterances it was not because they did not know how to make complex utterances, for example by using *but* and *because*. They did not examine possibilities frequently, but it was not because they did not have ready access to *perhaps*, and *might*. The evidence from the longitudinal study indicates that the children in the disadvantaged groups used these features less extensively than the children in the advantaged groups, because the purposes for which they generally expected to use language did not require them. All the children in the disadvantaged groups showed that they had an adequate vocabulary and a knowledge of linguistic structures, which they were able to draw on when pressed, or when their own need to be explicit made them essential. The children in the disadvantaged groups produced lower mean scores on utterance length and complexity of structure, yet they showed that they could produce long elaborated utterances in some situations.

We are not inferring from this that children in the disadvantaged groups had knowledge and resources for using language equal to those of the children in the advantaged groups. Many were not fluent and groped for words, pressing words and structures into use haltingly. Others spoke readily enough in some situations but needed encouragement and support in others. The evidence indicates only that the children in the disadvantaged groups had greater resources of language than their typical performances revealed.

Children's Use of Language

The major difference between children in the advantaged and disadvantaged groups in the study was in their dispositions to use language for particular purposes. These differences were first evident in their talk when they were 3 years old as they played with a friend, and then at the ages of $5\frac{1}{2}$ and $7\frac{1}{2}$ there were important differences in the way in which children responded to the devised interview situations. In these interviews, whereas children in the advantaged groups anticipated the kind of appropriate response expected by the interviewer, children in the disadvantaged groups tended to produce very short responses that were often of a different character from the responses that would be expected by teachers as appropriate answers.

At the age of 3 the children in the disadvantaged groups were not using language spontaneously for purposes that were already evident in the talk of the children in the advantaged groups. The disadvantaged groups showed little evidence of the use of language for:

recalling and giving detail of past experience;
reasoning about present and recalled experiences;
anticipating future events and predicting the outcome;
recognising and offering solutions to problems;
planning and surveying alternatives for possible courses of action;
projecting into the experiences and feelings of other people;
using the imagination to build scenes through the use of language for their play.

The talk of all the children in the advantaged groups showed that such uses of language were already developing.

At the ages of 5 and 7 years, situations were designed to stimulate responses that would indicate the child's disposition to use language for the purposes listed above. In all these situations the children in the disadvantaged groups produced much shorter responses, and the language used expressed a level of thinking that tended to be less complex than that expressed by the children in the advantaged groups. The children in the disadvantaged groups showed, through their use of language, that they were less aware of alternative interpretations, and were less inclined to project beyond the immediate requirements of the task.

It is, perhaps, important to reiterate the qualification to these conclusions, which we have made throughout our discussions. The limited responses, which were generally given by children in the disadvantaged groups, seem to indicate a lack of awareness, and restricted interpretations, but it could be that the responses represent not a lack of awareness, or limited thinking, but stem from attitudes that prevent them seeing the expression of their awareness, or their extended thinking, as appropriate or relevant.

It is not easy to judge which of these two explanations is the more likely. Frequently, when pressed further, the disadvantaged children gave fuller responses and moved towards the kind of answer given spontaneously by children in the advantaged groups. This could be seen as evidence that it was children's attitudes to the interview situation that prevented them from responding more fully, or it could be taken that the further questions and comments by the interviewer provoked them into awareness of those aspects that were neglected previously.

Although the outcome in school is likely to be the same whichever is the case, that is, the child is likely to be judged by his limited responses, recommendations about how to meet the problem might be conceived differently according to which interpretation is set upon the disadvantaged child's apparent inability to give fuller and more adequate responses. In the one view, increasing motivation to respond would be seen as the solution, whereas in the other view, more practice to make him familiar with what is required would be seen to be the solution. Although, as we have frequently stated, all the children seemed well motivated, and certainly were not reluctant to take part in the work, nevertheless it seems that an approach is needed through the establishment of a relationship with the teacher that the child finds supportive and satisfying, and through a choice of topics or situations that hold the child's attention and in which dialogue will seem relevant to his interests.

But there seems to be no doubt from these results that if education depends upon, or is based upon, the uses of language we examined, then those children whose fathers were unskilled and semi-skilled workers are likely to continue to be at disadvantage within school.

The Effects of Nursery Education

One aspect of the research had been to study the effects of two years' experience in a nursery school or class on the child's use of language.

As we read more widely and studied research that had examined children's development of language, we became more aware of the kind of experiences needed by children if skill in using language is to be developed, and therefore more aware of the problems of studying the effects of experiences in a nursery school or nursery class on children's development of language.

A further publication will be devoted to an examination of children's experiences at home that promote different skills and different attitudes in children and closer consideration will be given to the kind of experiences that promote reflectiveness and the extension of meanings that underlie explicitness and elaboration (Tough and Sestini, in preparation).

The children who formed the nursery groups were selected from eleven different nursery schools and classes and all were under the supervision of qualified teachers. The teachers were all aware of the importance of stimulating language development but there had not been, at that time, any investigation of ways of improving the quality of the interaction between teachers and children. A wide range of play experiences and many interesting situations were provided. Teachers and their helpers could be seen talking with children and offering beneficial experiences but generally they were not deliberately using strategies designed to promote particular skills of thinking and using language.

The study did not produce overwhelming evidence to show that experience in nursery schools and classes would reduce the problems of disadvantaged children at later stages. Nevertheless there was evidence to show that the children who had spent two years in a nursery school or class had made some gains.

The language used by the children in the nursery groups was not recorded until they were settled in school. The recordings were made, on average, six weeks after the children had started school. During this period the children gained experience of talking with adults in situations that were similar to the play situation in which their talk as they played with a friend was recorded. This seems to be the most likely explanation for the generally higher scores on all language measures for the disadvantaged group with nursery experience. Some of the differences between the mean scores of the nursery disadvantaged group and the non-nursery disadvantaged group were at a level of statistical significance beyond the 0·01 level.

The mean IQ for the two disadvantaged groups remained similar, although slightly higher for the nursery group, at $5\frac{1}{2}$ and $7\frac{1}{2}$. The differences between the scores on the verbal scale and on the performance scale at the age of 5 were less for the nursery group than for the non-nursery group and this was at the 0·01 level of significance. This might be interpreted as indicating that the children's potential as measured by the performance scale was more fully realised on the verbal scale.

The nursery disadvantaged group also had higher mean scores on all language measures at the age of $5\frac{1}{2}$, some of which were at a level of statistical significance. This is an indication that the disadvantaged children who came from nursery schools and classes had some advantage when they entered infant school. The results from the analyses of the children's use of language when they were 7 years old shows the mean scores of the nursery disadvantaged group to be generally higher than those of the non-nursery disadvantaged group, but the differences are no longer at a level of statistical significance.

There is some evidence then from the study to point to the possibility that nursery education has specific effects on the children's use of language. We are very much aware of the difficulties of isolating and measuring benefits, and recognise, in any case, that nursery education is concerned with a wider range of learning than we have considered. From the insight gained from our study it would seem, however, that if any gains from nursery experience are to be maintained when children enter infant classes they must meet conditions that will not only support their increasing skills but will actively extend them. We cannot expect progress to be maintained unless there is appreciation of the disadvantaged child's problems and efforts are made to promote his learning. Even if teachers are aware of the experiences that disadvantaged children need, we must not underestimate the difficulties of providing the kind of interaction needed by individual children when there are thirty or more in a class. But the results from the study indicate that if ways could be found to help children to develop skills in thinking and communicating in the nursery and infants' school, then positive gains might be achieved and maintained. The crucial question is concerned with changing priorities in allocating resources so that the essential skills that provide the basis for education can be established during the early years.

Education in Early Childhood: Some Conclusions

What, then, are the implications of our findings for the education of disadvantaged young children? An answer to this question necessarily depends on the way in which education is conceived, but in our view education for young children must be more than the acquisition of skills and knowledge. In our view education must be concerned with developing those skills and attributes that are important for benefiting from, and contributing to, life in the community and for participating in the decision-making processes of a democracy. Such objectives are concerned with self-discipline and responsibility, with self-confidence and self-expression, and with developing the ability to reflect, to analyse and to survey causes, to reason and anticipate possible consequences before taking action or reaching decisions. Basic to the development of these skills and attitudes is the motivation to think critically and to communicate effectively with others.

In education, then, the attitudes, and values that are promoted are as important as, and complementary to, the skills and knowledge that are accumulated. Above all, the development of a disposition to think, and reflect on experiences, provides an impetus towards the more effective use of skills, and greater understanding and appreciation of the knowledge and facts that are being acquired.

What part of this development can be promoted during early childhood? We have already demonstrated that the young child has a potential for using language and for developing ways of thinking critically about his experiences. Since these skills provide the basis, and the impetus, for developing further understanding, acquiring new skills and knowledge, and indeed cannot be fostered without gains being made on these other fronts, then the development and use of language must be seen not only as an objective for early childhood education, but as the major means through which other objectives for education may be reached.

Some children, as we have seen, already have well-developed skills in communicating when they come to school and they will, from the start, be in tune with teachers' expectations. Other children already have well-developed attitudes, towards adults and towards their own experiences, that may hinder them from responding and gaining skill in thinking and new understanding. Since these skills are so essential, not only for the child's education, but for the development of cognitive skills and social awareness, and for his development as a person, his early education must be directed towards helping him to realise the potential that he has for thinking and for communicating through the use of language.

Some attempts to meet the problems of the young disadvantaged child in school are now well known. Many have seen the problem as lying in the child's lack of knowledge of language, and have constructed programmes that are entirely devoted to, or contain a strong component of, language teaching. They concentrate on vocabulary building, the practice of syntactic structures and the use of locational prepositions, and although they may adopt different methods of presentation the goals are very similar. Some, like the Distar Programme, rely on syntactic patterning and repeated drills (Bereiter and Engelmann, 1969) as does the Peabody Language Development Kit (Dunn, Horton and Smith, 1968). Other programmes try to stimulate the extension of vocabulary and the employment of particular structures through interaction between children in structured situations as, for example, described in *Talk Reform* (Gahagan and Gahagan, 1972). The assumptions underlying the design of such programmes are that the disadvantaged child learns differently from others and that his knowledge of languge is deficient. The evidence of our longitudinal study suggests that the problem ought to be conceptualised differently.

THE ROLE OF DIALOGUE IN EARLY EDUCATION

We have not undertaken in this account the examination of the basis of experiences from which the child's orientation to use language develops. We have reserved this aspect for full discussion in a companion volume, *The Language of Mothers and Their Children* (Tough and Sestini, in preparation). But we cannot conclude without referring to the basis of experience from which the child will learn to think and communicate in particular ways.

All young children's learning is based on their own direct experiences. Learning to use language is no exception. Children learn to use language as they begin to communicate with others. Talking with others provides the model and the context and so forms the basis of experiences upon which the child's own disposition to use language will develop.

The most important experiences for the child's development of language and of thinking would seem likely to be the experiences he has of dialogue with others. Bruner has expressed the importance of dialogue quite clearly many times, for example:

> There are doubtless many ways in which a human being can serve as a vicar of the culture, helping a child to understand its point of view and the nature of its knowledge. But I dare say that few are so potentially powerful as participating in dialogue. (Bruner, 1971, p. 107)

But what does taking part in dialogue entail? What skills must the child develop if he is to enter into dialogue with others? In communicating we are trying to convey some meaning that resides within ourselves to others, and to receive meanings that reside within others. Even where people have well-developed skills of thinking and of using language, there are often misunderstandings, and patience and continued discussion, as well as a willingness and an ability to appreciate another's viewpoint, are necessary ingredients if mutual understanding is to be reached. The problem when we talk with the child is not only that his knowledge and skill in using language are immature, but that the kinds of meanings that he has so far developed are also immature.

What is it that the child must learn to do if he is to take part in dialogue, and what does he learn through the experience of participating in dialogue? The young child is still egocentric, that is, he cannot easily take the standpoint of others. But if he is to communicate effectively he must be able to anticipate the kind of information that should be made available to his listener. In our study, the disadvantaged children's failure to communicate effectively often seemed to be a failure of this kind: that is, they failed to recognise that there was essential information to be given if the listener was to understand the ideas being offered.

But projecting into the other's needs as listener is only part of the requirements of dialogue. The child must also reflect on his own meanings and find language to express the meaning that he is wanting to communicate. Every individual has within him what is described by Kellner as his own 'subjective texture of meanings' (Kellner, 1970) that develops from his past experiences. These are the meanings that he can turn to in order to find meaning for new situations. These are the meanings that he can draw on when he engages in dialogue. He must project into the other's viewpoint or needs as listener and then inspect his own meanings and draw from them what is needed to be made clear to the other, and find language to represent those meanings. According to Kellner, this provides the basis for the 'reciprocity of perspectives' needed in dialogue. In Mead's terms, those who engage in dialogue need to be 'taking the role of the other' (Mead (1934, 1964). If language is to provide a means of exchanging meanings, then those who communicate must project into the meanings of each other. Thus taking part in dialogue necessarily demands a projection into the perspective of the other, alternating with an inward reflection on the meanings that are to be offered to the other.

So we can see that if the child is to take part in dialogue he must learn to switch from giving attention to his own inner meanings to projecting into the meaning of others. This is not easy in the early years because the child is only just establishing his own viewpoints and cannot easily project and understand the view from another's angle. This is why talk between young children rarely takes on the character of dialogue because they are essentially egocentric and only with help can they consider other people's positions. That is not to say that there is no communication between young children. Communication goes on at different levels, and where experiences are mutually held it is not so dependent on the switch from self to another's meanings. Some kind of communication clearly goes on between children through the immediate activity. They confirm with one another what they have seen or done and direct their own and each other's actions. But this is communication of a different kind from that of expressing ideas drawn from experiences that are not held in common and are dependent on representation through language for the exchange of meanings.

Between adults who use language effectively, there can still be wide gaps in meanings, misunderstandings can, and often do, take place. But when the child and the adult talk there is likely to be a wider gulf between their meanings. This gap can only be reduced by the adult who can try to understand the child's view, to get inside him, as it were, and see his problems. The adult who understands what the child's problems in communication are is able to help the child by trying to give him the motivation he needs for expressing his ideas, and for helping him to appreciate the kind of information that the listener needs to be given, as well as helping the child to project into the adult's intentions and meanings as he listens to the adult's talk. What the adult expresses, and the way in which he expresses his meaning, must take account of the child's difficulties.

It is through the experiences gained with adults who take up a tutorial relationship with him that the child is gradually able to gain insight into the other's perspectives. In this relationship the child is continually helped to reflect on what he knows, to reconsider what he has said, to give attention to the essential elements of his experiences and try to put them into a structure. The child needs continual encouragement to make an internal inspection of his own experiences and ideas. The child also needs help if he is to project beyond himself and his own experiences. The tutoring adult helps by indicating the problems he has in understanding the child, giving the child clues to what further information is needed, and thus helping the child to build up strategies that are effective for communication. It is this continual alternation in dialogue between the inspection of one's own meanings and considering the problems of communication that seems to provide not only the basis from which the child will build knowledge of language and the skills of communication, but also the means of becoming reflective.

The character of reflection is that of inner dialogue. The self must take both parts in the dialogue, that of the self who is putting forward ideas, explanations, arguments, and that of the critical listener who questions and challenges, who provokes explanations and justifications. The tutoring adult must not only play the part of critical listener, and provide the model of responses for the child to take within, but must also demonstrate the character of *reflection* by expressing ideas, by offering information to the child and by engaging the child in thinking out loud. This seems to be the kind of experience from which the advantaged child has learned as he is drawn into discussion, and hears the 'thinking out loud' that goes on between members of the family. It may be an experience that is not met frequently by the disadvantaged child.

The skills that are developed through the experiences of participating in dialogue are those skills of thinking and using language that would seem to provide the very basis from which education can proceed. The disadvantaged child seems unlikely to establish these essential skills except through dialogue, and through dialogue with an adult who is aware of his problems and is deliberately providing experiences of dialogue through which new skills and attitudes may be learned.

It is important, then, to look at the contexts in which dialogue can go on in school. The teacher must aim at producing in the child self-motivation towards thinking and learning. This is not likely to happen if the teacher neglects the child's interest, and fails to engage him in activities that have interest for him. The natural environment, and the devised environment of school, should be used to challenge his interest and arouse his curiosity and promote a need to communicate.

LANGUAGE AND IMAGINATIVE PLAY

All nursery and infants' schools recognise that the child's play can provide an impetus towards learning, and play experiences are included as an essential part of the curriculum for young children. The use of language in imaginative play in which words are used to rename objects and construct events was one aspect where there were significant differences between the children in the advantaged and disadvantaged groups. The children in the disadvantaged groups used imagination as they played the roles of others, and renamed objects, for example calling a stick a 'gun'. They did not, however, build up the imagined scene using language as the sole or major means of representation. The readiness with which the children in the advantaged groups built up such imagined scenes, and the impetus that this provided for using language explicitly, emphasise the value that play holds for cognitive, as well as for social and emotional development.

Perhaps we have in the past regarded play as a part of children's development that is not learned, and the ability to play as inevitably unfolding as the children grew older. The differences that emerged between the groups of children in the study challenges our assumptions about play.

When does imaginative play being to appear? At quite an early age, perhaps in response to adults' or older children's suggestions, or by imitation of adults and older children. In many families parents encourage imaginative play, intuitively drawing their children into imaginative play by introducing ideas and materials to them. They do not explicitly teach them how to play imaginatively but they assume that this is a very suitable way for children to pass their time and many parents not only encourage imaginative play, but also actively promote it. Usually parents are not encouraging their children to play imaginatively because they think such activity will promote the growth of language and thinking: they do it because they are busy, and such play is likely to keep the child happily engaged for some time.

It seems likely, then, that where the child's imaginative play flourishes, he has been introduced by parents or older children to imaginative play experiences. These children then find the activity so rewarding that they return to it time and time again. Through play, children rework aspects of their experiences using the imagination to recreate and extend the possibilities of past events. Each time they play imaginatively language may be used in an explicit way to establish a scene for their play that others can share.

The disadvantaged children in the study did not extend their imaginative play through the use of words, as the advantaged children did. It seems that children who are at educational disadvantage may not have been involved in experiences that promote the use of language in imaginative play. If this is the case, then helping the child in the nursery to develop imaginative play seems likely not only to lead him to more satisfying play experiences but at the same time seems likely to exercise his thinking and his use of language. Such stimulation by the teacher should aim at enhancing the child's play so that he gradually learns to expect more from play himself. The teacher's intervention should not destroy the child's imaginative play but support and extend it where appropriate. The use of language in imaginative play seems likely to bring its own rewards through the extension of the play experience so that the child begins to incorporate ideas and uses of language as he plays when the teacher is not supporting him. In this way language seems likely to come to be used explicitly and to serve the child's own purposes, in addition to providing access to new ways of thinking.

THE ENABLING ENVIRONMENT

Play is only one of the activities in which the child's use of language can be fostered in school. Children are essentially curious and want to explore materials, and use them to construct and represent. They are interested in a whole range of natural phenomena. They are interested in other people and their behaviour. The enabling environment seems likely to be one that encompasses activities that are likely to gain the child's interest and so ensures motivation for thinking and understanding. Such activities provide a potential basis for meanings to be developed, provide the context in which dialogue can become rewarding to the child, because it brings new understanding and a new mastery of the world around him.

Extending the child's thinking in situations that are meaningful and satisfying to him seems likely to be the best way of ensuring that the skills of thinking and of using language will become a resource that the child will begin to use increasingly for the value it has for him. If thinking and communicating skills are to benefit the child's life outside school then it is important that new skills should become part of the child's disposition towards all his experiences. It is important then that the motivation to think and communicate should arise both from satisfying relationships with others and from the relevance of the child's own activities.

The teacher needs then to develop a knowledge of language and skills of communication so that the child's thinking and use of language can be deliberately influenced through dialogue. For this an ongoing analysis of both the child's and the teacher's use of language is needed. The interpretation of these principles and the translation into classroom practice is discussed in *Focus on Meaning* (Tough, 1973a) and *Listening to Children Talking* (Tough, 1976) and *Talking and Learning* (Tough, in preparation).

The child is dependent on the skills of the teacher and on the view that the teacher takes of him. The disadvantaged child's potential may be overlooked and unfulfilled because school fails to provide him with the experiences he needs in order to establish the kind of perspective on his experiences, and the skills of communication, from which his education can flourish.

The most important help that we can give to young children in school is likely to be through those experiences that foster the potential they have for using language as a means of thinking and communicating; in this way those children who are at disadvantage when they come to school might develop new ways of interpreting their experiences and new meaning for their time in school.

Appendix

Table 1. *Mean age and mean IQ of groups and subgroups at time of first recording*

Groups and subgroups	Mean age in months when recorded	Mean IQ (SB 1961)	Number in group
Advantaged groups			
Nursery girls	39·0	128·5	6
Nursery boys	39·0	129·5	6
All nursery	39·0	129	12
Non-nursery girls	38·0	127	6
Non-nursery boys	40·0	129·5	6
All non-nursery	39·0	128·3	12
All advantaged	39·0	128·7	24
Disadvantaged groups			
Nursery girls	41·0	128·3	6
Nursery boys	38·0	125	6
All nursery	39·5	126·7	12
Non-nursery girls	41·0	124·2	6
Non-nursery boys	39·0	126·5	6
All non-nursery	40·0	125·4	12
All disadvantaged	40·0	126·1	24

Table 2. *Analysis of length of utterances*

Group and subgroups	Mean length of all utterances	Mean length of 5 longest utterances	Number of utterances 8 words and longer	Number of 8+ utterances as % total all utterances
Advantaged groups				
Nursery girls	6·2	15·1	158	24·6
Nursery boys	5·9	15·4	182	20·9
All nursery	6·0	15·2	340	22·5
Non-nursery girls	5·3	13·3	105	14·0
Non-nursery boys	5·7	12·4	121	18·2
All non-nursery	5·5	12·8	226	16·0
All advantaged girls	5·7	14·2	263	18·9
All advantaged boys	5·7	13·8	303	19·7
All advantaged	5·7	14·0	566	19·0
Disadvantaged groups				
Nursery girls	4·5	10·6	79	8·3
Nursery boys	4·0	8·3	26	2·8
All nursery	4·3	9·4	105	5·6
Non-nursery girls	3·4	6·9	13	1·7
Non-nursery boys	3·8	7·5	16	2·0
All non-nursery	3·6	7·2	29	1·9
All disadvantaged girls	4·1	8·8	92	5·5
All disadvantaged boys	3·9	7·9	42	2·4
All disadvantaged	4·0	8·3	134	3·9
*Level of significance of differences between the advantaged and disadvantaged groups	$p = 0.001$	$p = 0.01$	$p = 0.01$	

* This table gives only the mean score for each subgroup, but comparisons in the study are all based on the mean scores for individual children. The Mann–Whitney U test (Siegel, 1956, p, 116), a test based on rank order of scores, was applied to test the level of significance between the scores of children in the advantaged and disadvantaged groups.

Table 3. *Use of complexity of structure*

Group and subgroups	Total utterances	Compound utterances	Complex utterances	Elaborated utterances	Total complex + elaborated utterances	No. clauses
Advantaged groups						
Nursery girls	642	16	49	11	60	59
Nursery boys	870	30	64	15	79	85
All nursery	1512	46	133	26	139	144
Non-nursery girls	749	14	33	8	41	40
Non-nursery boys	663	9	46	8	54	52
All non-nursery	1412	23	79	16	95	92
All advantaged	2924	69	212	42	234*	236*
Disadvantaged groups						
Nursery girls	950	15	23	1	24	25
Nursery boys	940	3	12	0	12	12
All nursery	1890	18	37	1	38	37
Non-nursery girls	734	1	10	0	10	10
Non-nursery boys	787	2	5	0	5	5
All non-nursery	1521	3	15	0	15	15
All disadvantaged	3411	21	52	1	53*	52*

* Level of significance between advantaged and disadvantaged groups, using χ^2 test for two independent samples $p=0.001$.

Scoring guide for Noun Phrase Index (after Cazden, 1965)

N = noun   poss = possessive
A = article   Ma = any modifier other than an article
pl = plural   prep = preposition

Score 1
(a) N: dog
(b) N + N: school dress

Score 2
(a) A + N: a cat
(b) Ma + N: black line
(c) N + pl: cars
(d) N + poss: mummy's
(e) 1 + prep: to bed

Score 3
(a) A + Ma + N: a different piece
(b) A + N + pl: some flowers
(c) Ma + N + pl: tiny bits
(d) N + poss + N: sister's coat
(e) A + N + poss: the dog's
(f) 2 + prep: into heaps

Score 4
(a) Ma + Ma + N: great big car
(b) A + Ma + N + pl: some beautiful patterns
(c) A + N + poss + N: the doctor's car
(d) Ma + N + poss + N: funny clown's nose
(e) 3 + prep: from baby's mouth

Score 5
(a) Ma + Ma + N + pl: beautiful new shoes
(b) A + Ma + Ma + N: a big yellow bird
(c) N + poss + N + pl: father's pipes
(d) A + Ma + N + poss + N: the nice lady's hat
(e) N + poss + Ma + N: mummy's red dress
(f) 4 + prep: to the girl's house

Score 6
(a) A + Ma + Ma + Ma + N: a great big fat man
(b) A + Ma + Ma + N + pl: some pretty blue flowers
(c) 5 + prep: with a funny green spot

Scoring guide for Verb Complexity Index

Score 1
Imperative (Vi): Get off.

Score 2
Unmarked verb (Vum): You have one.
Gone, got: You got a bed now.
Unmarked auxiliary (Aux. um): I can, you do.
Infinitive (Inf.): You to go there dolly.
Question form (?)

Score 3
Present participle (VPrp): You going to bed.
3rd person singular present (V3p): The snow comes down.
Marked auxiliary (person): I am, he has (Aux.p).
                 (past):   You were, he had. (Aux.past).
Regular past (V.Reg.p): Oh dropped my baby.

Items scoring 1 plus 2
    Vi + Vum: Come look.
    Vi + gone, got: Get done.
    Vi + Inf.: Go to sleep.

Score 4
Marked auxiliary (future): I will. (Aux.f).
                (conditional): I might. (Aux.c).
Irregular past (V.Irreg.p): I gave her a pink thing.

Items scoring 1 plus 3
    Vi + VPrp: Get going fire tractor.
    Vi + V.Reg.p: Get killed.
    Vi + Inf.: Try to make it.

Items scoring 2 plus 2
    Vum + Vum: Hear it crack.
    Got, gone + Inf.: He got to look at it.
    Aux.um + Vum: I can go home.
    Aux.um + gone, got: I've got my baby to bed.
    Inf. + Vum: Batteries – to make it go.
    Aux.um + ?: Can I? Do you?
    Vum + ?: Have you a car?

Score 5
Items scoring 1 plus 2 plus 2
    Vi + Vum + Vum: Let me make it stick on.
    Vi + Vum + Inf.: Come try to find it.

Items scoring 1 plus 4
    Vi + V.Irreg.p: Get it found.

Items scoring 2 plus 3
> Vum + VPrp: You try painting a picture.
> Aux.um + V.Reg.p: I have turned the taps off.
> Got + V.Reg.p: He got killed.
> Inf. + VPrp: Car to start going now.
> Vum + V.Reg.p: You get washed.

Items scoring 3 plus 2
> Vprp + Inf.: Going to come down.
> V.Reg.p + Vum: I helped it walk.
> VPrp + Vum: You going find him.
> V3p + Inf.: She wants to sit up.
> V3p + Vum: It makes my arm look nice.
> Aux.p + Inf.: He has to go home.
> Aux.past + Inf.: He had to go home.
> V.Reg.p + Inf.: . . . that's why I wanted to skip.
> Aux.p + ?: Is he?
> Aux.past + ?: Had I? Did you? Was she?

Score 6

Items scoring 1 plus 2 plus 3
> Vi + Vum + VPrp: Let me try sticking it on.
> Vi + Inf. + VPrp: Try to go swimming.
> Vi + Vum + V.Reg.p: Let him get bathed.

Items scoring 2 plus 2 plus 2
> Aux.um + Vum + Inf.: I can try to skip.
> Aux.um + gone, got + Vum: I've got hurt.
> Aux.um + gone, got + Inf.: I've got to see you.
> Aux.um + Inf. + Vum: I want to make it jump.
> Aux.um + Inf. + Inf.: We have to ring up to wake the fire brigade.
> Aux.um + Inf. + ?: Have we to ring you?
> Aux.um + Vum + ?: Can I try?
> Aux.um + got + ?: Have you got some more toys?

Items scoring 3 plus 3
> V3p + VPrp: It keeps doing it.
> Aux.p + VPrp: He is coming down now.
> Aux.past + V.Reg.p: He had bumped his head.
> V.Reg.p + VPrp: She stopped crying then.
> V3p + V.Reg.p: My little tich gets covered up.
> Aux.p + VPrp I am putting this in.

Items scoring 2 plus 4
> Aux.um + V.Irreg.p: I have bought a car.
> Got + V.Irreg.p: I got brought home.
> Vum + V.Irreg.p: You get sent to hospital.

Items scoring 4 plus 2
> Aux.c + Vum: I might go with you.
> V.Irreg.p + Inf.: He came to mop it up.
> Aux.c or f + ?: Might you? Will he?

Score 7

Items scoring 1 plus 2 plus 2 plus 2
    Vi + Vum + Inf. + Vum: Let me try to help you stick it.
    Vi + Vum + Inf. + Inf.: Do try to learn to swim.

Items scoring 1 plus 3 plus 3
    Vi + VPrp + VPrp: Try learning swimming.

Items scoring 2 plus 2 plus 3
    Get + Inf. + VPrp: You got to try pushing it.
    Vum + Vum + VPrp: He can go swimming.

Items scoring 3 plus 4
    Aux.past + V.Irreg.p: It was bought for me.
    Aux.p. + V.Irreg.p: It is given to me.
    V3p + V.Irreg.p: It looks broken.

Items scoring 3 plus 2 plus 2
    Aux.p got, gone + Vum: She has got hurt.
    Aux.p + Inf. + Inf.: He has to go to see.
    Aux.p + Vum + Inf.: The doctor has come to see you.

Items scoring 4 plus 3
    V.Irreg.p + VPrp: He came running down the road.

Items scoring 2 plus 2 plus 3
    Aux.um + got + V.Reg.p: I've got a thingummy tied in to there.
    Aux.um + Vum + VPrp: I can hear them shouting.

Items scoring 2 plus 3 plus 2
    Aux.um + V.Reg.p + ?: Have you mended it?
    Aux.um + V.Reg.p + Inf.: They have tried to go.

Items scoring 3 plus 2 plus 2
    Aux.p + Inf. + ?: Is he to go now?
    Aux.past + gone + ?: Had he gone then?

Score 8

Items scoring 4 plus 2 plus 2
    Aux.f + Vum + Inf.: Now this will have to have it.
    Aux.c. + Vum + Inf.: I'd have to have my dinner.
    Aux.f. + Aux.um + gone: Then you will be gone.
    Aux.c. + Aux.um + got: Then you might have got it.
    Aux.c. + Aux.um + Inf.: A bit of wire would do to fasten this.
    Aux.c. + Aux.um + Vum: Well daddy might have come with her.

Items scoring 3 plus 3 plus 2
    Aux.p + VPrp + Inf.: I'm just going to put the telephone back.
    Aux.p + VPrp + ?: Are you going now?
    Aux.p + V.Reg.p + Inf.: He's supposed to go.

Items scoring 3 plus 2 plus 3
    Aux.p + got + VPrp: Well, if it's got smoke coming out of it.
    Aux.p + gone + VPrp: He has gone swimming.

Items scoring 2 plus 2 plus 2 plus 2
> Aux.um + got + Inf. + ?: Have you got to go with these little things?
> Aux.um + gone + Inf. + ?: Have you gone to see it?

Items scoring 2 plus 4 plus 2
> Aux.um + V.Irreg.p + Vum: I've made it go further.

Score 9
Items scoring 3 plus 3 plus 3
> Aux.p + Aux.past + VPrp: It has been spoiling all the rest.
> Aux.p + V.Reg.p + VPrp: It has stopped snowing.
> Aux.p + VPrp + V.Reg.p: It is getting mended.

Items scoring 4 plus 2 plus 3
> Aux.c + Aux.um + V.Reg.p: Police car could be fastened.

Items scoring 3 plus 2 plus 4
> Aux.p + got + V.Irreg.p: This one's got broken.

Items scoring 3 plus 2 plus 2 plus 2
> Aux.past + Aux.um + Inf. + ?: Did we have to have it?

Items scoring 3 plus 4 plus 2
> Aux.p + V.Irreg.p + ?: Is it broken?

Items scoring 4 plus 2 plus 3
> Aux.f + Aux.um + V.Reg.p: Mother will have turned round.

Score 10
Items scoring 3 plus 2 plus 3 plus 2
> Aux.p + Vum + V.Reg.p + ?: Does it come undressed?

Items scoring 3 plus 3 plus 2 plus 2
> Aux.p + VPrp + Inf. + Vum: And he's going to let go.

Items scoring 2 plus 2 plus 2 plus 2 plus 2
> Aux.um + Vum + Inf. + V.Reg.p + ?: Do you want to get bathed?

Score 11
Items scoring 3 plus 3 plus 2 plus 3
> Aux.p + VPrp + Inf. + V.Reg.p: She's going to get dressed.

Items scoring 4 plus 2 plus 3 plus 2
> Aux.c + Aux.um + VPrp + Inf.: She might be going to ring N. up.

Items scoring 3 plus 3 plus 3 plus 2
> Aux.p + VPrp + V.Reg.p + ?: Is it getting dressed?

Table 4. *Analysis of complexity in noun and verb phrases and of the use of pronouns*

Groups and subgroups	1 Noun Phrase (instance) Index	2 Noun Phrase (opportunity) Index	3 Reference Index	4 Verb Complexity Index
Advantaged groups				
Nursery girls	2·21	1·22	23·02	4·45
Nursery boys	2·33	1·34	23·56	4·10
All nursery	2·28	1·29	23·30	4·25
Non-nursery girls	2·10	1·08	17·34	4·45
Non-nursery boys	2·17	1·06	19·91	4·38
All non-nursery	2·14	1·07	18·64	4·41
All advantaged girls	2·16	1·15	20·18	4·45
All advantaged boys	2·25	1·20	21·73	4·24
All advantaged	2·22	1·18	20·97	4·35
Disadvantaged groups				
Nursery girls	2·14	0·90	9·65	3·64
Nursery boys	2·05	1·08	10·01	3·73
All nursery	2·09	1·03	9·83	3·68
Non-nursery girls	1·72	0·67	4·76	2·79
Non-nursery boys	1·82	0·70	5·47	3·09
All non-nursery	1·77	0·68	5·12	2·95
All disadvantaged girls	1·92	0·81	7·20	3·21
All disadvantaged boys	1·93	0·90	7·74	3·41
All disadvantaged	1·92	0·86	7·5	3·31
*Level of significance of differences between the advantaged and the disadvantaged groups	$p = 0.002$	$p = 0.001$	$p = 0.001$	$p = 0.001$

* This table gives only the mean score for each subgroup, but comparisons in the study are all based on the mean scores for individual children. The Mann–Whitney U test (Siegel, 1956, p. 116), a test based on rank order of scores, was applied to test the level of significance between the scores of children in the advantaged and disadvantaged groups.

NB

1   The Noun Phrase (instance) Index is the mean scores of all noun phrase scoring using the system given on page 183.

2   The Noun Phrase (opportunity) Index takes the scores of all noun phrases and the mean is calculated for all reference points, that is for the total number of nouns and pronouns.

3   The Reference Index is the expression of all anaphoric pronouns (that is where the pronoun refers to a noun present in the utterance) as a percentage of all pronouns used.

4   The Verb Complexity Index is the mean score of all verb complexes scoring using the system given on page 184.

Table 5. *Analysis of the use of language by 3-Year-Olds*

	Advantaged groups			Disadvantaged groups		
	Nursery	Non-nursery	All advantaged	Nursery	Non-nursery	All disadvantaged
I Self-monitoring	81	119	200*	293	225	518*
II *Directive* (a) monitoring own actions	145	130	275*	497	567	1064*
(b) extending action and collaborating in action	66	23	89*	27	7	34*
III *Interpretative* Present (a) identifying	183	207	390*	416	577	993*
(b) extension through ref. to detail, etc.	197	171	368	145	84	229
(c) logical reasoning	68	82	150*	18	1	19*
Past (a) identifying	29	25	54	6	4	10
(b) extension through ref. to detail	44	20	64*	5	2	7*
(c) towards logical reasoning	25	18	43*	6	0	6*
IV *Projective* 1 Predictive	63	79	242	74	32	106
2 Empathetic	8	5	13	1	0	1
3 Imaginative (a) directive in	227	264	491	256	89	345
(b) extending actions	425	238	663*	107	13	120
(c) identifying; representation	26	54	80	45	10	55

Table 5 (*cont.*)

	Advantaged groups			Disadvantaged groups		
	Nursery	Non-nursery	All advantaged	Nursery	Non-nursery	All disadvantaged
(d) extension of imagined context	40	100	140*	30	10	40*
(e) towards logical reasoning in imagined context	29	23	52*	4	0	4
(f) role taking	49	26	75	113	2	115
Total projective			1756			786

* Categories in which one group scored twice as often as the other.
** Categories in which one group scored at least three times as often as the other.

Table 6. *Mean IQ of groups of children at three ages**

Groups and subgroups	Stanford Binet at age 3	WISC at age 5½	WISC at age 7½
Advantaged groups			
Mean age	3 years 3 months	5 years 5 months	7 years 4 months
Nursery girls	126·8 (8)	123·3 (8)	123·2 (8)
Nursery boys	128·1 (8)	122·8 (6)	120 (7)
All nursery	127·5 (16)	123·1 (14)	121·6 (15)
Non-nursery girls	124·3 (8)	120 (8)	122·2 (7)
Non-nursery boys	126·0 (8)	122·3 (8)	120 (8)
All non-nursery	125·1 (16)	121·1 (16)	121·1 (15)
All advantaged	126·3 (32)	122·1 (30)	121·3 (30)
Disadvantaged groups			
Mean age	3 years 4 months	5 years 6 months	7 years 6 months
Nursery girls	126·1 (8)	118 (8)	113·3 (8)
Nursery boys	122·7 (8)	119 (8)	113 (8)
All nursery	124·4 (16)	118·5 (16)	113·1 (16)
Non-nursery girls	123·4 (8)	115·3 (8)	112·3 (7)
Non-nursery boys	124·2 (8)	113·2 (7)	111·2 (7)
All non-nursery	123·8 (16)	114·2 (15)	111·6 (14)
All disadvantaged	124·1 (32)	116·3 (31)	112·4 (30)

* Figures in brackets indicate numbers of children available at time of testing from original groups selected at the age of 3.

Bibliography

BERKO, J. (1958), 'The Child's Learning of English Morphology', *WORD*, 14

BEREITER, C. and ENGELMANN, S. (1966), *Teaching Disadvantaged Children in the Pre-School*, New Jersey: Prentice Hall

BERNSTEIN, B. (1958), 'Some Sociological Determinants of Perception: An inquiry into subcultural differences', *British Journal of Sociology*, 9, 2

BERNSTEIN, B. (1961), 'A Theory of Social Learning' in *Education, Economy and Society*, ed. Halsey, Froud and Anderson, Illinois: The Free Press of Glencoe

BERNSTEIN, B. (ed.) (1971), *Class, Codes and Control: Vol. 1, Theoretical Studies Towards a Sociology of Language*, London: Routledge and Kegan Paul

BERNSTEIN, B. (1973a), 'A Brief Account of the Theory of Codes' in *Social Relationships and Language*, ed. V. Lee, Bletchley: The Open University

BERNSTEIN, B. (1973b), *Class, Codes and Control: Vol. 2, Applied Studies Towards a Sociology of Language*, London: Routledge and Kegan Paul

BROWN, R. (1958), *Words and Things*, New York: The Free Press of Glencoe

BROWN, R., CAZDEN, C. B. and BELLUGI, U. (1969), 'The Child's Grammar from I to III' in R. Brown, *Psycholinguistics*, New York: The Free Press (1970), pp. 75–9

BROWN, R., FRASER, C. and BELLUGI, U. (1963), 'Control of Grammar in Imitation, Comprehension and Production' in R. Brown, *Psycholinguistics*, New York: The Free Press (1970), pp. 28–55

BROWN, R., FRASER, C. and BELLUGI, U. (1964), 'Explorations in Grammar Evaluation' in R. Brown *Psycholinguistics*, New York: The Free Press (1970), pp. 56–74

BROWN, R. and HANLON, C. (1970), 'Derivational Complexity and Order of Acquisition in Child Speech' in *Cognition and the Development of Language*, ed. J. K. Hayes, New York: Wiley

BRUNER, J. S. (1964), 'The Course of Cognitive Growth', *American Psychologist*, 19, 1–5

BRUNER, J. S. (1971), *The Relevance of Education*, London: Allen and Unwin

BRUNER, J. S., OLVER, K. and GREENFIELD, P. (1966), *Studies of Cognitive Growth*, New York: Wiley

BUTCHER, H. J. (1968), *Human Intelligence*, London: Methuen

CAZDEN, C. B. (1965), 'Environmental Assistance to the Child's Acquisition of Grammar, doctoral dissertation, Harvard University

CHOMSKY, C. (1969), *The Acquisition of Syntax in Children from 5 to 10*, Cambridge, Mass.: MIT Press

CHOMSKY, N. (1965), *Aspects of the Theory of Syntax*, Cambridge, Mass.: MIT Press

CICOUREL, A. V. (1973), *Cognitive Sociology*, London: Penguin

DEUTSCH, M. P. (1965), 'The Role of Social Class in Language Development', *American Journal of Orthopyschiatry*, 35, 78–88

DOUGLAS, J. W. B. (1964), *The Home and the School*, London: MacGibbon and Kee

DOUGLAS, J. W. B., ROSS, J. M. and SIMPSON, H. R. (1968), *All Our Future*, London: Peter Davies

DUNN, L. M., HORTON, K. B. and SMITH, J. O. (1968), The Peabody Language Development Kit, American Guidance Service, Circle Pines, Minn.

EWING, A. W. C. (ed.) (1957), *Educational Guidance and the Deaf Child*, Manchester University Press

FIRTH, J. B., cited by Hymes (1964), 'Toward Ethnographics of Communication', *American Psychologist*, **66**, 3, p. 2

FURTH, H. (1966), *Thinking Without Language*, Illinois: The Free Press of Glencoe

GAHAGAN, D. M. and GAHAGAN, G. A. (1970), *Talk Reform*, London: Routledge and Kegan Paul

GOLDMAN-EISLER, F. (1968), *Psycholinguistics: Experiments in Spontaneous Speech*, London: Academic Press

HALLIDAY, M. A. K. (1973), *Exploration in the Functions of Grammar*, London: Arnold

HASAN, R. (1968), *Grammatical Cohesion in Spoken and Written English Part 1*, Nuffield Programme in Linguistics and English Teaching Paper No. 1, London: Longmans

HAWKINS, P. R. (1969), 'Social Class, the Nominal Group and Reference', *Language and Speech*, **12**, 2

INHELDER, B. and PIAGET, J., 1959 (1964), *The Early Growth of Logic in the Child*, London: Routledge and Kegan Paul

JACOBSON, R. (1960), 'Linguistics and Poetics' in *Style and Language*, ed. T. A. Sebeok, New York: Wiley

KELLNER, H. (1970), 'On the Sociolinguistic Perspective of the Communication Situation, *Social Research*, **37**, 71–8

KOHLBERG, L. (1963), 'Development of Children's Orientations Towards a Moral Order: Sequences in the development of moral thought', *Vita Humana*, 6

LABOV, W. (1970), 'The Logic of Nonstandard English' in *Language and Poverty*, ed. F. Williams, New York: Markham Press

LENNEBERG, E. H. (1962), 'Understanding Language Without the Ability to Speak: A case report' *Journal of Abnormal and Social Psychology*, **65**, 419–25

LENNEBERG, E. H. (1965), 'The Natural History of Language' in *The Genesis of Language*, ed. F. Smith and G. A. Miller, Cambridge, Mass.: MIT Press

LEWIS, M. M. (1951), *Infant Speech*, London: Routledge and Kegan Paul

LEWIS, M. M. (1957), *How Children Learn to Speak*, London: Harrap

LEWIS, M. M. (1968), *Language and Personality in Deaf Children*, Slough: NFER

LURIA, A. R. (1959), 'The Directive Function of Speech in Development and Dissolution', *WORD*, **15**, 3, pp. 341–52; reprinted in R. C. Oldfield and J. C. Marshall, *Language*, Harmondsworth: Penguin (1968)

LURIA, A. R. (1961), *The Role of Speech in the Regulation of Behaviour*, Harmondsworth: Penguin

LURIA, A. R. and YUDOVITCH, F. I. (1959), *Speech Development and Mental Processes in the Child*, London: Staples

MCNEIL, D. (1966a), 'The Creation of Language', *Discovery*, **27**, 7, p. 34

MCNEIL, D. (1966b), 'The Creation of Language by Children' in *Psycholinguistic Papers*, ed. J. Lyons and R. Wales, Edinburgh University Press

MCNEIL, D. (1970), *The Acquisition of Language*, New York: Harper Row

MEAD, G. H. 1934 (1964), 'Mind' in *George Herbert Mead on Social Psychology*, ed. A. Strauss, Chicago and London: University of Chicago Press

MENYUK, P. (1963), 'Syntactic Structures in the Language of Children', *Child Development*, **34**, 2, pp. 407–22

MOORE, T. (1967), 'Language and Intelligence: A longitudinal study of the first eight years: Part 1, Developmental Patterns of Boys and Girls', *Human Development*, 2, pp. 1–24

MOORE, T. (1968), 'Language and Intelligence: A longitudinal study of the first eight years: Part 2, Environmental Correlates of Mental Growth', *Human Development*, 2, pp. 1–24

OGDEN, C. K. and RICHARDS, I. A. (1923), *The Meaning of Meaning*, London: Routledge and Kegan Paul

OLERON, P. (1956), *Recherches sur le développement mental des sourds-muets*, Paris: CNKS

PIAGET, J. (1923, rev. edn 1959), *The Language and Thought of the Child*, New York: Harcourt, Brace and World

PIAGET, J. (1932), *The Moral Judgement of the Child*, London: Routledge and Kegan Paul

PIAGET, J., 1941 (1952), *The Child's Conception of Numbers*, New York: Humanities Press

PIAGET, J. (1954), 'Language and Thought from a Genetic Point of View' in *Acta Psychologica* 1954, **10**, 88–98; and in *Psychological Studies*, ed. D. Elkind, New York: Random House

PIAGET, J. (1962), *Comments on Vygotsky's Critical Remarks Concerning 'Language and Thought of the Child' and 'Judgement and Reason in the Child'*, Cambridge, Mass.: MIT Press

PIAGET, J. and INHELDER, B. (1966), *Mental Imagery in the Child*, London: Heinemann

ROBINSON, P. (1972), *Language and Social Behaviour*, Harmondsworth: Penguin

ROSEN, H. (1972), *Language and Class*, Bristol: Falling Wall Press

SAMPSON, O. C. (1956), 'A Study of Speech Development in Children 18–30 Months', *British Journal Educ. Psychology*, **26**, 3, pp. 194–201

SAPIR, E. (1921), *Language: An Introduction to the Study of Speech*, New York: Harcourt, Brace and World

SKINNER, B. F. (1957), *Verbal Behaviour*, New York: Appleton Century-Crofts

SLOBIN, D. I. (1971), *Psycholinguistics*, Illinois: Scott, Foresman

SMITH, M. E. (1935), 'A Study of some Factors Influencing the Development of the Sentence in Pre-school Children', *Journal of Genetic Psychology*, **46**, 182

STRICKLAND, R. (1962), 'The Language of Elementary School Children', *Bulletin of School of Education*, Indiana University, **38**, 4

TEMPLIN, M. C. (1957), *Certain Language Skill in Children*, Oxford University Press

TOUGH, J. (1973a), *Focus on Meaning*, London: Allen and Unwin

TOUGH, J. (1973b), Children's Use of Language, *Educational Review*, **26**, 3

TOUGH, J. (1976), *Listening to Children Talking*, London: Ward Lock

TOUGH, J. (in preparation), *Talking and Learning*, London: Ward Lock

TOUGH, J. and SESTINI, E. (in preparation), *The Language of Mothers and Their Children*

VINCENT, M. (1957), 'The Performance of Deaf and Hearing Children on a Classifying Task', **10**

VYGOTSKY, L. S., 1934 (1962), *Thought and Language*, Cambridge, Mass.: MIT Press

WHORF, B. (1941), 'The Relation of Habitual Thought and Behaviour to Language' in *Language in Thinking*, ed. P. Adams, Harmondsworth: Penguin (1972)

WHORF, B. (1956), *Language, Thought and Reality*, Cambridge, Mass.: MIT Press

WISEMAN, S. (1964), *Education and Environment*, Manchester University Press

Index